We Are Pen Women

Santa Clara County Branch
1922 - 2022

Luanna K. Leisure

We Are Pen Women
Santa Clara County Branch
1922 - 2022

Copyright © 2022

ISBN: 978-0-578-38296-8

Published by Luanna K. Leisure, Campbell, California 95008

Luanna K. Leisure, Little White Feather Graphic Artist and Independent Publisher.

Printed in the United States of America.

We Are Pen Women painting on the front cover, page 75, and page 137 by Pen Woman Dorothy Atkins, San Jose, California 95132

Sri's Daughter, painting page two, Girl in the Garden painting on page four by Pen Woman Judith Tolley, San Jose, California 95131

We Are Branches painting on page ten by Pen Woman Carol Brolin, Palo Alto, California 94301

Centennial Owl painting on pages xiv, 24, 76, and back cover by Pen Woman Phyllis Gunderson, Pecos, New Mexico 87552

Most photographs throughout the book were randomly taken by Pen Women Patricia Dennis and Luanna Leisure

To order books go to: http://www.LuLu.com or Amazon.com

Email: NLAPWSantaClara@aol.com

Contents

Contents

Contents

Dedication

This book is dedicated to the amazing founders of the National League of American Pen Women who paved our way, to Pen Women of today, and to those who will carry on our mission.

Appreciation

Much appreciation and gratitude goes to Mary Miller Chiao, Carol Green, Carolina Mueller and Winifred Thompson. Each volunteered for different tasks that took hours and hours of their time to edit and proof our book. These ladies have been a priceless asset to the quality of our book. Others donated their art, poetry, photos, made calls and helped with research. Every single member has been involved in one way or another.

Special Thank You!

Jill Adler, Modesto Branch
Dorothy Atkins
Carol Brolin
Mary Miller Chiao
Patricia Dennis
Carol Greene
Phyllis Gunderson
ShaRon Haugen
Herb Leisure
Carolina Mueller
Winifred Thompson, Diablo-Alameda Branch
Judith Tolley
Evelyn Wofford, National President
Susan Zerweck

Thank you, Pen Women for taking the time to write your bios. Thank you Evelyn Wofford, our National President, for searching files in D.C. and for answering my many questions.

Luanna K. Leisure
Santa Clara County Branch President

A Note from National President
Evelyn Wofford

It is with a great deal of pleasure that I congratulate the Santa Clara County Branch of the National League of American Pen Women, Inc., on the occasion of its one hundredth anniversary. The League was chartered and incorporated in 1897 in Washington, D.C. Its purpose then, as it is now, was to provide support to professional women writers, visual artists, and musicians and to encourage the production of quality endeavors in these fields both within and outside the organization. When Santa Clara County Branch was chartered in 1922, only 12 branches had been chartered previously. These branches stretched from Los Angeles and San Francisco to Miami and Western New York and from Mobile to Kansas City. The League at that time was called simply "League of American Pen Women." This name did not change until December, 1926, when it became the National League of American Pen Women, Inc. Three other branches were chartered in 1922, and of the four, only Santa Clara County remains. That fact indicates the resilience and determination of the founding members of this branch and all of you who are now upholding the tradition of the seventeen charter members of this organization. They were tenacious women who were determined to take or make a place for themselves in the male dominated world in which they found themselves. Much has changed in society over the last one hundred years, or one hundred twenty-five years since the League's founding, but much remains to be done. It is wonderful to know that the women of Santa Clara County Branch of the NLAPW remain dedicated to making our society better through the arts.

A Note from Branch President
Luanna K. Leisure

I cannot fully express how much I have enjoyed being Branch President. Zoom has been a blessing in the midst of Covid-19, allowing us to continue our regular meetings as well as meet more often with special Zoom events. Your presentations and demos have been wonderful. I've loved hearing about your accomplishments in your unique fields. You're an amazing group of ladies, and I continue to learn from you.

It has been delightful working with branch members gathering documents and photos for our 100 year anniversary book. In reading the biographies, I've been privileged to become better acquainted with each one of you. I hope you will enjoy our 100 year anniversary book and that it will be kept as a part of our Pen Women history. It's a work of love and a gift of appreciation to my family of sisters in the Santa Clara County Branch.

My first love is being the Scholarship Chair. I so enjoy the fruits of our labors in presenting our monetary awards to talented young women in the arts who are pursuing their educations. My first contact with Pen Women was over 30 years ago when I met some lovely ladies providing scholarships in Visalia, California.

Being National Membership Development Chair has opened my eyes to the accomplishments as well as the needs of our branches nationwide. I am inspired by our members and I am learning from our branch presidents.

The Membership Committee is composed of a core who hold up my arms and give me inspiration and strength. Together with Winifred Thompson, Jill Adler, Usha Shukla, Ruey Syrup, Dorothy Atkins, and Patty Kennedy; we brainstorm ideas, organize meetings with other branches, and always work together with positive and uplifting attitudes.

I want to give a shout out to Laura Walth who organizes Zoom meetings for our Members-at-Large. I have met so many marvelous women whom I otherwise would have never had the opportunity to meet.

I also want to thank National President Evelyn Wofford, who has been so kind to me. Evelyn's help and guidance has been priceless. She is always there for me.

In summary, I feel so very privileged to be a Pen Woman.

.

A Note from Branch Vice-President
Patricia Dennis

Throughout my life I have been affiliated with many groups, all of which have had positive effects on my life. With NLAPW, I found a purpose not only in contributing to the branch but also from receiving continuing support.

Every member has made a significant positive impact on how I address my art and writing and how I give back! With their support and guidance, I have had the confidence to take on board roles as well as develop the Santa Clara County Branch website and assist with the scholarship awards program as co-chair and Art Chair.

With each scholarship the branch awards, there comes a feeling of pride as we watch young hopefuls stand up and face us. With our scholarships, we inspire young ladies to pursue their goals. They worked hard for this first step! We give them an opportunity to see the advantages of being a part of our 'tribe' and also at a national level that has endured for years. What a wealth of information there is at our fingertips through this League! Writers, Artists, Musicians, we are all sisters under one umbrella.

Thank you Santa Clara County Branch members for giving me the security of being involved with a tribe of like-minded creative women and the comfort in knowing that on some level we all understand each other and are proud to call one another sisters.

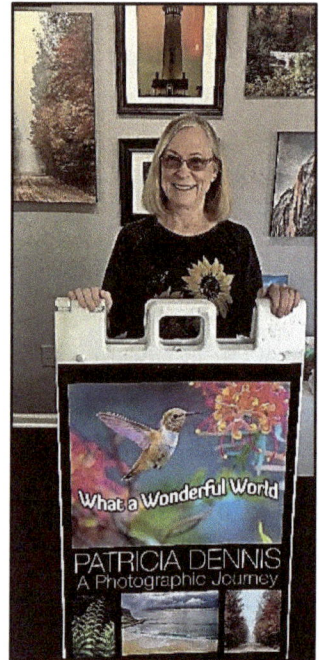

A Note from NorCal President
Dorothy Atkins

I am proud and honored to serve as NorCal President to the Santa Clara County, Diablo-Alameda, Modesto, Golden Gate-Marin, and Stockton-Lodi Branches. Yearly, NorCal branches host two meetings that bring our branches together. Due to Covid, our in-person meetings and shows were moved to Zoom.

Recently, our member, Claudia Gray, represented our branch in the NorCal Art show held at the Lindsay Dirkx Brown Gallery. As the Outreach Chair, our "Socks for Cold Feet" campaign collected over 500 pairs of socks for the homeless.

During the summer, with the Stockton-Lodi Branch and members-at-large we co-hosted our first very popular Summer Read. In addition, our branch came together to share our stories and accomplishments in a highly spirited Zoom meeting which kept us connected.

This year, we had the opportunity to partner with the San Jose Woman's Club via Zoom with presentations by Louise Webb and me. My presentation discussed racial unrest in our country. Louise Webb presented a riveting presentation about interviewing famous stars; and our entire branch showcased their creativity with their accomplishments. The spirit and collective creativity of our members unite us in a way that keeps our branch strong and connected.

Pen Arts Building

Headquarters, National League of American Pen Women, Inc.

1300 17th Street NW, Washington, D.C. 20036

Santa Clara County Branch
www.NLAPWsantaclara.org
Email: NLAPWSantaClara@aol.com

1922 2022
SCC Branch 100 years

NLAPW Washington, D.C.
www.NLAPW.org
Email: NLAPW1@gmail.com

National League of American Pen Women

Linking Creative Women Since 1897

We are professional writers, poets, journalists, painters, sculptors, photographers, dancers, musicians, choreographers, art teachers, theater and film directors — and creatives in many other fields.

We are about 1,200 members across the United States in 57 branches.

Our Mission is to encourage, recognize, and promote the production of creative work of professional standard through outreach activities, provide educational, creative, and professional support to members and nonmembers.

Our core values are respect, knowledge, creation and preservation of the arts.

Centennial Owl
By Phyllis Gunderson
Oil on Linen
10 x 8 x 5

National League of American Pen Women
Santa Clara County Branch
1922 – 2022
Celebrating 100 Years

Our Santa Clara County branch is one hundred years old and still growing strong in spite of Covid-19, while the world, literally the whole world, has been devastated and ripped apart from an invisible invader. The pandemic has separated us physically, but now we have been drawn even closer together through advances in technology that we would never have imagined twenty years ago. We can still hold our meetings on Zoom. We hold virtual art shows, demonstrations and readings. We have the delightful ability to meet with our NorCal sisters much more often. Even beyond that, our branch Outreach Program and the National Membership Development Committee connects us on Zoom with Members-at-Large and with branches across the United States. No longer do we feel like we are a lone branch, but now we have been given a broadened perspective about how we are connected with our many sister branches around the country as well as with National headquarters in Washington, D.C.

Yes, we are in challenging times. Our sister Pen Women were in challenging times in 1897. We have different challenges; but as Pen Women, we are strong. What makes us different? What makes us strong? Is it the individual artistic talents we all have? Is it because, even though we are unique individuals, we have much in common and are supportive of each other's creativity? Whatever it is, let's keep doing it. Let's keep creating and encouraging one another. Let's continue to reach out to non-members, new members, and potential members. National has been doing this for 125 years, and now we have for 100 years. There is no end to our potential.

Luanna K. Leisure
SCC Branch President

Sri's Daughter
by Jude Tolley
Oil 16 x 20

There's Beauty in a Woman
by Susan Zerweck

There's beauty in a woman,

There's music in her soul,

There's beauty in a woman,

That soul that makes her whole.

It's not what's on her face

Or the way she does her hair.

The loveliness inside

Is what make a woman fair.

There's beauty in a woman

In the art that she creates.

There's beauty in a woman,

Art the viewer celebrates.

It's not the everyday

The mundane, the weary or the strife,

But how she goes beyond

Bringing joy and radiance to life.

There's beauty in a woman

In the talent deep inside.

There's beauty in a woman,

Talent nothing in the world can hide.

Susan Zerweck, a Pen Woman member for 31 years, is our Santa Clara County Branch Parliamentarian, Achievers Chair, National Commemorative Endowment Appointee, past branch President, and much more.

Girl in the Garden
by Jude Tolley
Oil on canvas

Reprint article from The Pen Woman Magazine January 1964. A history of the Santa Clara County Branch.

Forty Years as Happy Members of the Santa Clara County Branch, Founded March 5, 1922

EVA SKERRY-OLSEN

In the year 1922, Santa Clara Valley, California, was a panorama of blossoming orchards, flower and fruit, and vineyards marching up and down low hills, against a background of mountains, green in the spring and golden in the fall. Here and there among the orchards and vineyards nestled homes with palm-tree-lined approaches. And never was the sky so blue.

Into this paradise of fruitfulness came an inspired writer, Katherine Dunlap Cather, who at that time was collaborating with David Starr Jordan, of Stanford University, in an endeavor to bring to children a measure of his scientific knowledge in simple language. Katherine Cather was also writing "Girlhood Stories of Famous Women" and "Boyhood Stories of Famous Men." She had been a member of the San Francisco Branch of the League and yearned for the companionship of other writers here in Blossom Valley. Together with Grace Hyde Trine, a writer of pageants, they called together a nucleus of writers and artists in this area, with the idea of starting a new Branch.

Mary Jane Hoffman in costume of French housewife.

The first meeting was held on March 5, 1922, in the historic home of Edwin Markham on South Eighth Street, San Jose. Katherine Carter and Grace Hyde Trine told the assembled writers and artists of the National League of American Pen Women; its qualifications for membership, its vision and its achievements in the then 25 years of its accomplishments, and of their own happy experiences as members. The enthusiasm of the group was instantaneous, and after poring over applications and waiting

Edwin Markham House

fifteen breathless days, word came from Washington that the League had fourteen new members. The Santa Clara County Branch was launched. The organization meeting, on March 23rd, chose Katherine Dunlap Cather as president. Her initial talk gave a vision of the aspirations of the new group—that, in addition to having the honor of being a part of a great organization, we are also something unique in ourselves, for it is what we make of ourselves that counts toward the uplifting of both. "Let us enjoy a fellowship that sets us apart, while being in association with a great body of artists who see and project that which is beautiful."

Gertrude B. Murphy
Voted most outstanding member with most achievements to her credit.

The fourteen charter members were Katherine Cather; Pauline Hunt, of Los Gatos, who wrote children's stories for John Marten; Marjory Fisher; Elva Sawyer Cureton; Edith Daley, poet and city librarian; Mrs. Paul Clark (Pawnee Indian Stories); Mayo Hayes and Ruth Amet of the *Mercury Herald*; Ada Jane Kimball, *Evening News*; Katherine Kennedy; Clara Louise Lawrence, poet and children's stories; Anna Rozilla Crever, poet; Mildred Hamilton, public relations; and Jessie Del Enright, feature writer, of Santa Cruz.

At the first regular meeting, plans were made for a Book Fair, which turned out to be breathtaking in its scope. Never before had so many notable writers gathered in the west; Kathleen and Charles Norris, Esther Birdsall Darling, Gracy Hyde Trine, Alice McGowan and Perry Newberry, James Swinnerton and his wife Louise Scher; Anna De Neal Morgan, Gerald Beumont, the Freeman Olders, Ruth Comfort Mitchell, and a host of others. Never before or since has there been such a display of rare old volumes and fine book bindings. For two days and two nights the old Hotel Vendome was crowded with book-lovers, and witty writer-talk flowed over the banquet tables. Local stores devoted complete windows to the Fair—newspapers ran editorials of commendation.

Right on the heels of the Book Fair, Marjorie Fisher, chairman of a group of Little Theatre, sponsored, in the interest of children, "Snow White" and "Little Red Riding Hood," produced by Vivian Amet Johnson. Jimmie Swinnerton gave a chalk talk, and Bess and Don Richards produced "The Little Tin Soldier." Children were entertained at a nominal fee, and new talent was discovered. The Branch broke even in the venture.

That first year in October came a memorable luncheon at the Hotel Vendome. Esther Birdsall Darling of Berkley was the guest speaker. In November, the group gave $50.00 to the Community Chest. In December, another memorable luncheon, this time at the Stanford University Union, with James Swinnerton, Phinester Proctor, the sculptor, and Pedro Lemos, the artist, as guest speakers.

During Katherine Cather's second term as president came many outstanding affairs, such as entertaining our first national president, Grace Gelbert, in June, 1923. A motor tour through Blossom Valley preceded a luncheon at the Country Club; a reception was held in the afternoon at the Hotel Vendome, and a dinner followed.

For two years the new Branch did amazing things under the leadership of Katherine Dunlap Cather. Then a seeming tragedy happened—our extremely talented president and founder was called to New York and asked to be relieved of her office. While in New York in February, 1926, death overtook her, and she never returned to the valley she loved. The membership was appalled at its loss.

Meanwhile, a young and modest newspaper writer, who had been accepted into the Branch and had attended one meeting, was unaware that the woman sitting beside her in the office was the recently appointed chairman of the nominating committee. At the very next meeting the young woman found herself president of the Branch! To add to her consternation she soon found that each one of the other members had been urged to take the office—but all had refused—since no one dared follow the popular and exceedingly successful organizer. Stunned, the young woman shouldered the responsibility, and did a fine job. Sybil Hayes is still an active and much-loved member and only recently has retired from newspaper work and a daily radio broadcast of her fine inspiring thoughts. Today, she tells me modestly, that after her term the Branch has never found any trouble in finding presidents.

Sybil's leadership carried on with most interesting lectures on drama and ceramic art—and then the Branch went on the air with 26 half-hour programs on the romance of Santa Clara Valley. Gertrude B. Murphy was radio chairman, and Alma Lowry Williams was chairman of music. These plays were sponsored by the San Jose Chamber of Commerce, and produced by the students of San Jose State College. Pen Women writers were Ruth Comfort Mitchell, Ednah Aiken, Mrs. Freemont Older, Dana Lyon, and Margaret Craven. These plays were very popular.

In 1924, Mrs. J. O. Hayes and Marjorie Fisher were named delegates to the national convention in Washington.

That was the beginning. Since then the Santa Clara County Branch has grown and prospered and contributed in many ways to the cultural beauty of our valley, and has given fellowship and inspiration to its members, and an outlet for many talents. We have sponsored young talent with scholarships and San Jose State College, held many Art Fairs and outstanding programs at lovely Montalvo in Saratoga-the estate of former Senator James D. Phelan, which was willed by him as a cultural center.

Perhaps one of our most artistic contributions was an Art Tea in 1932-33 when Mary Jane Hoffman was our president. The setting was Pompeiian and given in the Pompeii Court of Hotel St. Claire. It came complete with costumed dancers and the music of a harpist. The pillars were covered with climbing ivy, potted flowering plants and palms on the low platform; statues of satyrs and Hermes in the background; tables decorated with laurel, sacred to Apollo. Jane Campbell Higbe, a professional decorator of our membership, who had just returned from a visit to Pompeii, gave a most interesting talk on the ancient life of the city. Vivian Amel Johnson produced poses from Pompeiian friezes and a ballet which began with the worship of Apollo and ended with the flight from the city during the time of the eruption of Vesuvius.

Perhaps, in looking over the achievements of our Branch, its far-reaching hospitality has been one of the most lasting of our contributions. Each year, for many years, we have given our now widely known Celebrity Luncheon. On these occasions, outstanding writers and artists and musicians have come to us as speakers and performers, and guests from many places in the Bay Area and beyond it, and have been entertained in our homes and enjoyed a community breakfast before returning home. Each year new writers and artists who have entered the professional field that year are sought out and acknowledged by name at the luncheon.

Many fine writers, artists and composers of music have come and gone among us during the years. Among them, Josephine Hughston, creative newspaper writer, and famous for her dinner parties, her hospitality and her great humanitarianism, was one of the most inspiring and diligent contributing members of the Branch during the early years. Kathleen Norris was once a member of our Branch. Ruth Comfort Mitchell, (novelist and wife of Senator Sanborn Young) was one of our outstanding early members. They lived in the hills above Los Gatos. Among her novels were "A White Stone," "Army with Banners," "Call of the House," "The Wishing Carpet," and also "Narratives of Verse." She was one of our presidents. Mrs. Fremont Older, wife of the editor of the *San Francisco Bulletin,* one of the most outstanding American editors of his time, wrote "California Missions and Their Romances," and "Love Stories of Old California."

Ednah Aiken, prominent in literary circles in the 1920's and 30's author of "Love and I" published by Dodd, Mead, and one of our presidents, contributed much to our Branch.

In going through the long records of our Santa Clara County Branch, I find most often the name of Gertrude B. Murphy, not only as a past president and continual contributor to the culture of the group by her excellent programs and her grace as our MC on our most outstanding affairs, but heading so many of our committees that represent many hours of time, talent, judgment, and downright labor. We choose her unanimously as our most outstanding contributor to the culture and happiness of this group.

Now, forty years after our charter, our Blossom Valley and the vineyard hills, to a great extent, have given place to the result of their own charms, and lovely California ranch houses march up and down the hills and spread themselves among the orchards and vineyards that still remain. Our Branch now has 45 members and two other branches have grown out of it. We still have with us four beloved and still very active members of those who gathered with enthusiasm under the leadership of Katherine Dunlap Cather in 1922. Forty years of fellowship, encouragement and cultural advancement has been our story, and we give our deep gratitude and our honor and loyalty to those who were our national founders and all those who now are its progeny. A long life N L A P W!

Markham House

The very first meeting of the National League of American Pen Women, Santa Clara County Branch was held on March 5, 1922, in the historic Victorian home of the famous poet, Edwin Markham, where he lived in the late 1800s. The house was moved from South Eighth Street, San Jose to History Park in San Jose. Poetry Center San Jose owns the refurbished house where they hold their meetings and events.

Pen Woman, Mary Lou Taylor is a member of Poetry Center San Jose. She held a publicity photo shoot at the Markham House for her poetry book, *Bringing Home the Moon*. Photographs taken by Luanna K. Leisure.

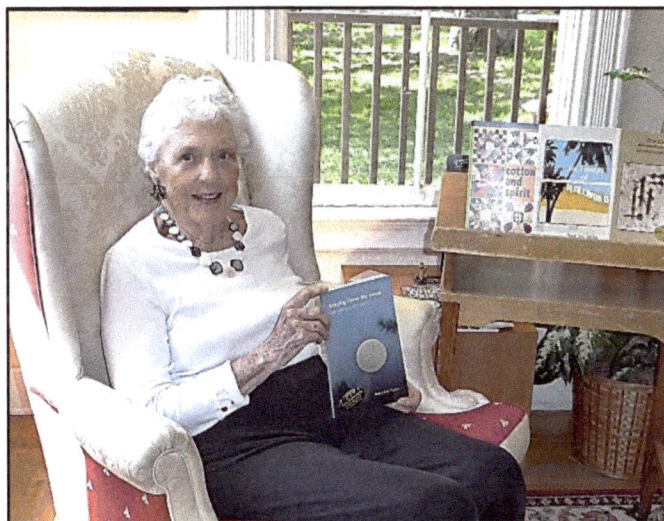

We are Branches
by Carol Brolin
Pen, Ink and Markers

We Are Branches

Have you ever wondered why we are called branches instead of clubs or chapters? I have, and I have not found any documentation stating why. I'm sure this was decided long ago, but I can certainly understand why.

A healthy tree will have deep roots, a sturdy trunk with strong limbs and branches. Each branch is unique and different. Depending on the variety of the tree, the branches will yield a variety of beautiful flowers, fruits and foliage.

This is how we are in the NLAPW. Each Branch is unique with unique members. Our flowers, fruit and foliage are our talented and gifted ladies in Letters, Music, and Art.

Think of the roots and trunk of a tree as our charter members who dug in deep with their heels, refusing to give up, determined to grow and endure the struggles they faced for equal rights. Because of their tenacity we can enjoy being the branches of their tree. We need to remember how Pen Women came to be. We are the strong branches with beautiful fruit, flowers and foliage. Let's keep growing.

~ Luanna K. Leisure

Coins Minted
In 1922

Twenty Dollars Gold	One Dollar Gold Commemorative	One Dollar

Half Dollar Ulysses S. Grant Commemorative	One Cent

A Few Historical Events
1921 - 1922

1921 **P.E.N.** is a worldwide association of writers, founded in London in 1921 to promote friendship and intellectual co-operation among writers everywhere. The first PEN Club was founded at the Florence Restaurant in London on October 5, 1921, by Catherine Amy Dawson Scott.

1922 was unusual in the sense that no nickels, dimes, quarters or half dollars were minted. No cents were minted in Philadelphia for the first time since 1815. There were Commemorative Ulysses S. Grant half dollars and $1 gold pieces minted.

1922 A schoolteacher and wife, Bertha Knight Landes entered politics as one of the first female members of the Seattle City Council. She served for four years then became council president and eventually acting mayor when the city's mayor left town to attend the Democratic National Convention in 1924.

Prohibition (1919–1933)

Roaring Twenties (1920–1929)

The **Molly Pitcher Club** was formed as a women's organization to promote the repeal of Prohibition in the U.S.

September 22, 1922 United States, and subject to its jurisdiction, are citizens thereof The Act of September 22, 1922, provided that "a woman citizen of the United States shall not cease to be a citizen of the United States by reason of her marriage."

Charter Members
Santa Clara County Branch
March 1922

Katherine Cather
Pauline Hunt
Marjory Fisher
Elva Sawyer Cureton
Edith Daley
Mrs. Paul Clark
Mayo Hayes
Ruth Amet
Ada Jane Kimball
Katherine Kennedy
Clara Louise Lawrence
Anna Rozilla Crever
Mildred Hamilton
Jessie Del Enright

Santa Clara County Branch Presidents

Founder
Katherine Dunlop Cather
1922-25

Sibyl Hayes 1925-1926
Elita Huggins 1926-1927
Ruth Comfort Mitchell 1927-1928
Marjory Fisher 1928-1929
Ednah Aiken 1929-1930
Gertrude B. Murphy.. 1930-1931
Bernice Downing 1931-1932
Mary Chancy Hoffman 1932-1933
Mildred Hamilton 1933-1934
May Hayward Killam 1934-1936
No record or roster for 1936-1938
Alma Lowry Williams 1938-1942
Pearl H. Simpkins 1942-1944
Ann Nash 1943-1945
Lutherian Cunningham Puccinelli (Habback) 1944-1946
Dorothy Kaucher 1946-1948
Jean Erskin Scott.. 1948-1950
Catherine Urban.. 1950-1952
Elain Davis... 1952-1954
Mildred Kaucher... 1954-1956
Ruth Reese 1956-1958
Borgehild O. Haugen 1958-1960
Vema Moxley Smith 1960-1962
Emma D. Chittick 1962-1964
Gertrude B. Murphy... 1964-1966
Helen Martin 1966-1968
Elita Huggins 1926-1927
Alice R. Shannon 1968-1970
Irene M. McDonald 1970-1972

Santa Clara County
Branch Presidents Continued

Phyllis McCallum	1972-1974
Mary Madge Saksena	1974-1976
Charlotte Dunn	1976-1978
Nettie Tays Campbell	1978-1980
Mary Chancy Hoffman	1980-1982
Alma Merrick Helms	1982-1984
Margery Dorian	1984-1986
Catherine Doris Pierce	1986-1988

Presidents' Photos and Terms in Office

Thyra Tegner
1988-1990

Doris Simmons
1990-1992

Doris Phifer
1992-1994

Dorothy Goble
1994-1996

Felicia Pollock
1996-1998

Susan Zerweck
1998-2002

ShaRon Haugen
2002-2006

Christine Dargahi
2006-2010 Co-Pres

Dianne MacNair
2006-2010 Co-Pres

Dorothy Atkins
2010-2013

Judy Bingman
2013-2016

Kathryn Tyler
2016-2018

Luanna Leisure
2018-2022

Officers and Committee Chairs
2018-2022

Susan Zerweck, Parliamentarian, Membership, Achievers; **Cyra Cowan**, Luncheon Chair; **Dorothy Atkins**, Community Outreach; **Luanna Leisure**, President, Roster, Branch Email News, Scholarship Chair; **ShaRon Haugen**, Treasurer; Historian, Roster; **Patricia Dennis**, Vice President, Publicity, Webmaster, Co-Scholarship Chair (2018-2021), Birthdays; **Marcia Sivek**, Secretary (2018-2021).
Not in above Photo: **Mary Miller Chiao**, Secretary (2021-2022);
Barbara Chamberlain, Sunshine Greetings.

Tina Jones Williams, Co-Scholarship Chair (2022)

A stroll through time with photos. The following pages are photos of events and meetings of our Santa Clara County Branch. We currently have 57 members; but because of Covid-19, we are meeting on zoom until members feel safe to meet in person.

Pen Women Meeting
C. 2005
Library in San Jose

Left to right back row: Ursula Meier, Susan Zerweck, Dianne MacNair, Carol Brolin, Christine Dargahi.
Middle row: Name Unknown, ShaRon Haugen, Carol Greene, Geraldine Scaife, Maria Chaviel, Audry Lynch Name Unknown, Toni Hird.
Front: Felicia Pollock, Tola Minkoff, Dorothy Goble.

NLAPW Meeting
Show & Tell
October 6, 2018

Top middle group picture back row: Marcia Sivek, ShaRon Haugen, Susan Zerweck, Claudia Gray, Katy Tyler, Judy Bingman, Kay Duffy, Jude Tolley, Bonnie Vaughan, Karen Franzenburg, Diana Chan, Annette Tan. **Middle row:** Tola Minkoff, Barbara Chamberlain, Cyra Cowan, Carol Brolin, Luanna Leisure, Dorothy Atkins, Nancy Bloomer Deussen. **Front row:** Patty Dick, Carol Greene, Lorna Kohler, Pat Fisher.

NLAPW Meeting
October 6, 2018
Show & Tell

**Carolina Mueller
Silk Art**

Carolina's Silk Art Demonstration
In Attendance
Carolina Mueller, Alice Ann Glenn, Patricia Dennis, Luanna Leisure, Jude Tolley, Dorothy Atkins, Tola Minkoff, Patty Dick, Sharon Haugen, Mary Miller Chio, Karen Franzenburg.

Home of Pat Fisher
Jan 5, 2019

Back row:
Katy Tyler, Jude Tolley, Karen Franzenburg, Judy Bingman, Dorothy Atkins, Susan Zerweck, Luanna Leisure.

Front row:
Pat Fisher (lower left), Barbra Chamberlain, Tracy Beardsley, Lorna Kohler, Patricia Dennis, Dorothy Brown.

Luncheon
May 4, 2019

Left to right and down the page:

Tina Jones Williams,
Jude Tolley,
Patricia Dennis,
Marcia Sivek,
ShaRon Haugen,
Carol Greene,
Judy Bingman,
Ariel's daughter,
Arial Smart,
Mary Lou Taylor,
Luanna Leisure,
Patricia Dennis,
Marcia Sivek,
Dorothy Atkins,
Pat Fisher,
Barbara Chamberlain,
Karen Franzenburg,
Ariel Smart,
Kay Duffy,
Nancy Bloomer Deussen,
Carol Greene,
Mary Miller Chiao,
Judy Bingman,
Maralyn Miller.

Meeting Luncheon
May 4, 2019

Rock Painting Party October 5, 2019
at the Home of Cyra Cowan
Organized by Patricia Dennis

Pat Fisher

Patricia Dennis

Cyra Cowan

Harriett Arnold

Jude Tolley

Luanna Leisure

Carol Brolin
Tola Minkoff

Louise Webb

Branch Meeting
January 9, 2020
At the Home of Patty Dick

Sharon Haugen, Norma Slavit, Alice Ann Glenn, Susan Zerweck, Jude Tolley, Tola Minkoff, Patricia Dennis, Gail Lockhart, Carol Brolin, Audry Lynch, Edie Matthews, Diana Chan, Patty Dick, Luanna Leisure, Dorothy Atkins, Pat Fisher.

Patty Dick and Patricia Dennis

Patty Dick, ShaRon Haugen, Patricia Dennis, Dorothy Atkins

Pandemic Strikes
Started Meetings on Zoom in 2020
Can't Keep Us Down

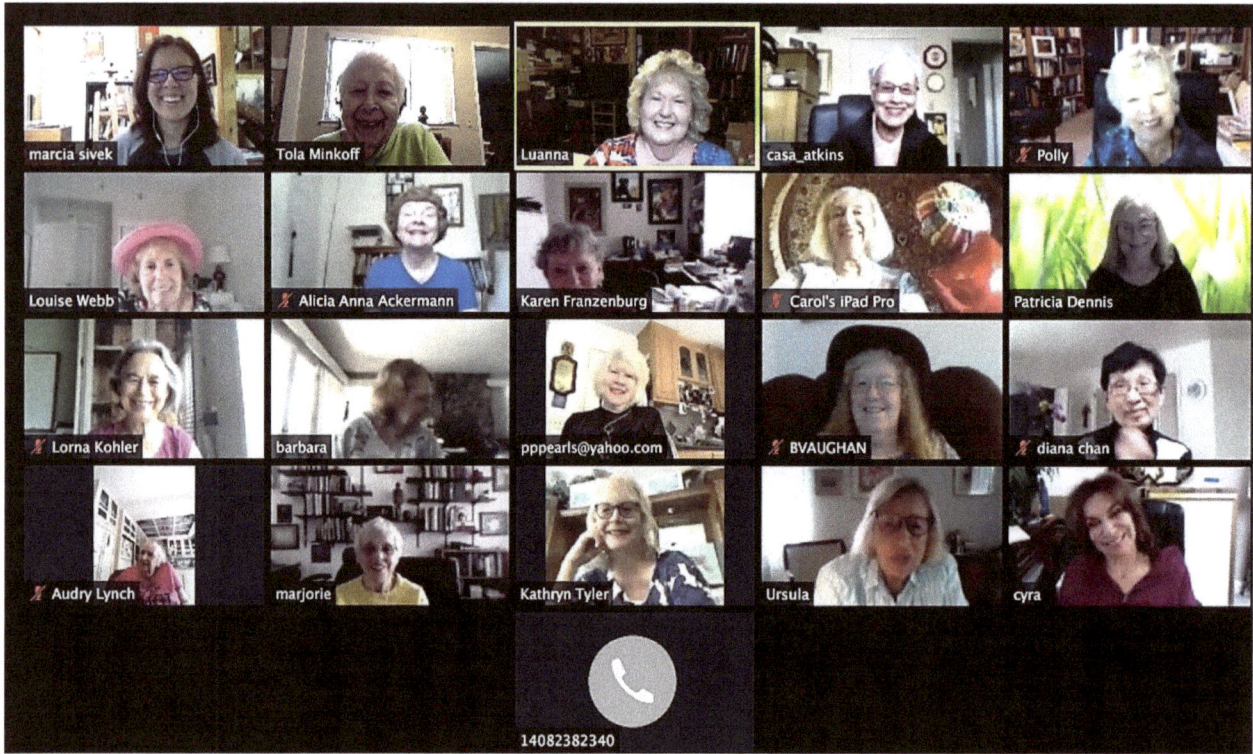

Summer Social
June 6, 2020

Top row left to right: Marcia Sivek, Tola Minkof, Luanna Leisure, Dorothy Atkins, Susan Zerweck. **Second row from top:** Louise Webb, Alice Ann Glenn, Karen Franzenburg, Carol Greene, Patricia Dennis. **Third row from top:** Lorna Kohler, Barbara Chamberlain, Patty Dick, Bonnie Vaughan, Diana Chan. **Bottom row:** Audry Lynch, Marjorie Johnson, Kathryn Tyler, Ursula Meier, Cyra Cowan, ShaRon Haugen on call in.

For a brief time we felt a little safer to meet in person as well as on zoom until the Delta variant hit.

Mix and Mingle
June 5, 2021
At Gail Lockhart's Studio

**Mix and Mingle at Gail Lockhart's
Stained Glass Studio**

Back row left to right top picture on left: Patty Dick, Tracy Beardsley, Will Lockhart, Gail Lockhart, Marjorie Johnson, Susan Zerweck, Mary Miller Chiao, Andy Deal, Name Unknown. Front row. Rolayne Edwards, Patricia Dennis, Audrey Wong, Luanna Leisure.

Picnic at Susan's

July 23, 2021

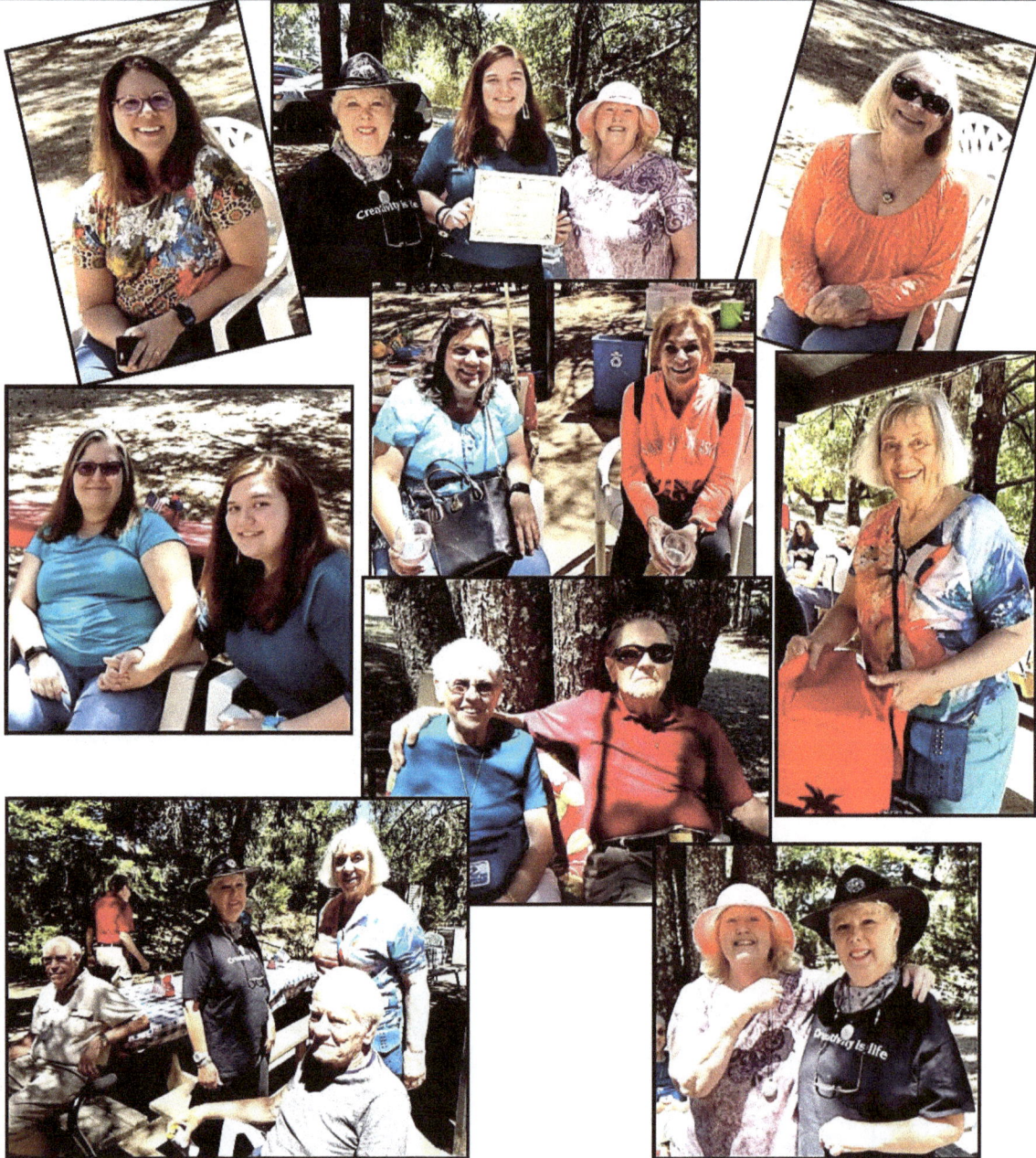

Picnic at Susan and Ralph Zerweck's
Honoring New Member Genevieve Liu

Top down left to right: Marcia Sivek, Susan Zerweck, Genevieve Liu, Luanna Leisure, Patricia Dennis, Susan Schmidt (Genevieve's mom), Genevieve Liu, Elvira Rascov, Cyra Cowan, Carol Greene, Marjorie Johnson, Bob Stetson, Paul Greene, Susan Zerweck, Carol Greene, Ralph Zerweck, Luanna Leisure, Susan Zerweck.

Lunch at Effie's
Honoring New Members
August 21, 2021

Celebrating New Members and Birthdays

Back row:
Patty Dick, Kristi Oberhauser, Lorraine Gabbert, Jude Tolley, Gail Lockhart.
Middle:
Marti Vaughan Northrup, Janie Oberhauser, Susan Zerweck.
Front:
Luanna Leisure, Tracy Beardsley, Patricia Dennis, Louise Webb.

Left:
Congratulations!
Janie Oberhauser

Center with Luanna Leisure & Susan Zerweck

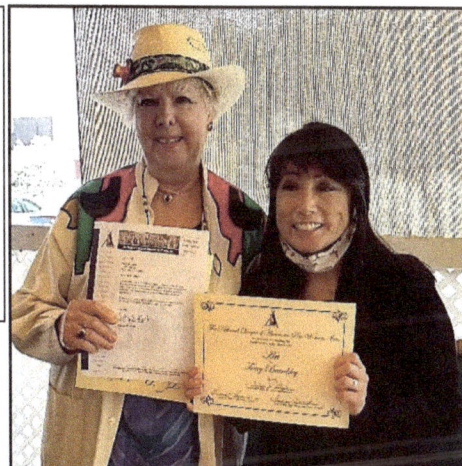

Above Right:
Congratulations!
Tracy Beardsley
with Susan Zerweck.

Bottom Left:
Happy Birthday Girls
Marti Vaughan Northrup, Patricia Dennis, Patty Dick, Janie Oberhauser and Jude Tolley

Zoom does not have to be boring.
We always like to make our meetings interesting.
A few examples

Zoom Kimekomi Japan
Doll Making Demonstration
by Tracy Beardsley
March 6, 2021

Voice of Women
Summer Read

Voice of Women - Summer Read
August 27, 2021

A delightful zoom, organized and hosted by Dorothy Atkins, our NorCal President, Santa Clara County Branch Outreach Chair, and Membership Outreach. The lineup was Pen Women from our Santa Clara County Branch, sister branches, a member-at-large and nonmember guests. All shared poetry or read from their books.

Left to right from the top down: Norma Slavit, Luanna Leisure, Dorothy Atkins, Marcia Sivek, Barbara Chamberlain, Harriett Arnold, Tola Minkoff, Cyra Cowan, Caroline Henry, Audry Lynch, Louise Webb, Vanice "Ann" Ellis, Mary Lou Mason, Elizabeth Yahn Williams, Tina Jones Williams, Darlene Weingand, Patricia Kennedy, Edie Matthews, Patty Watkins Dick, Elvira Rascov, Valia Clausell, Mary Miller Chiao, Carol Brolin, Parthenia Hicks, Carol Greene.

Zoom Collage Demonstration
by Lorraine Gabbert
October 2, 2021

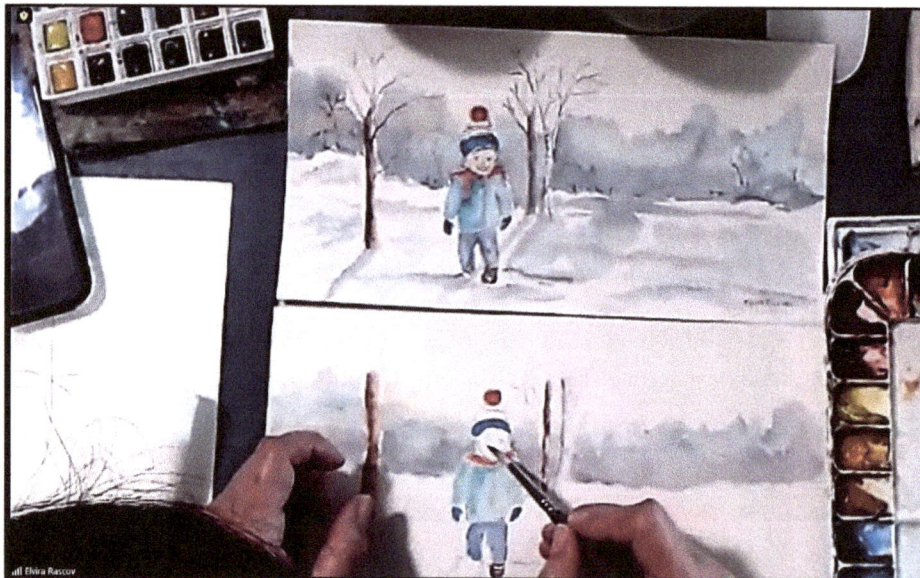

Zoom Watercolor Demonstration
By Elvira Rascov
January 1, 2022

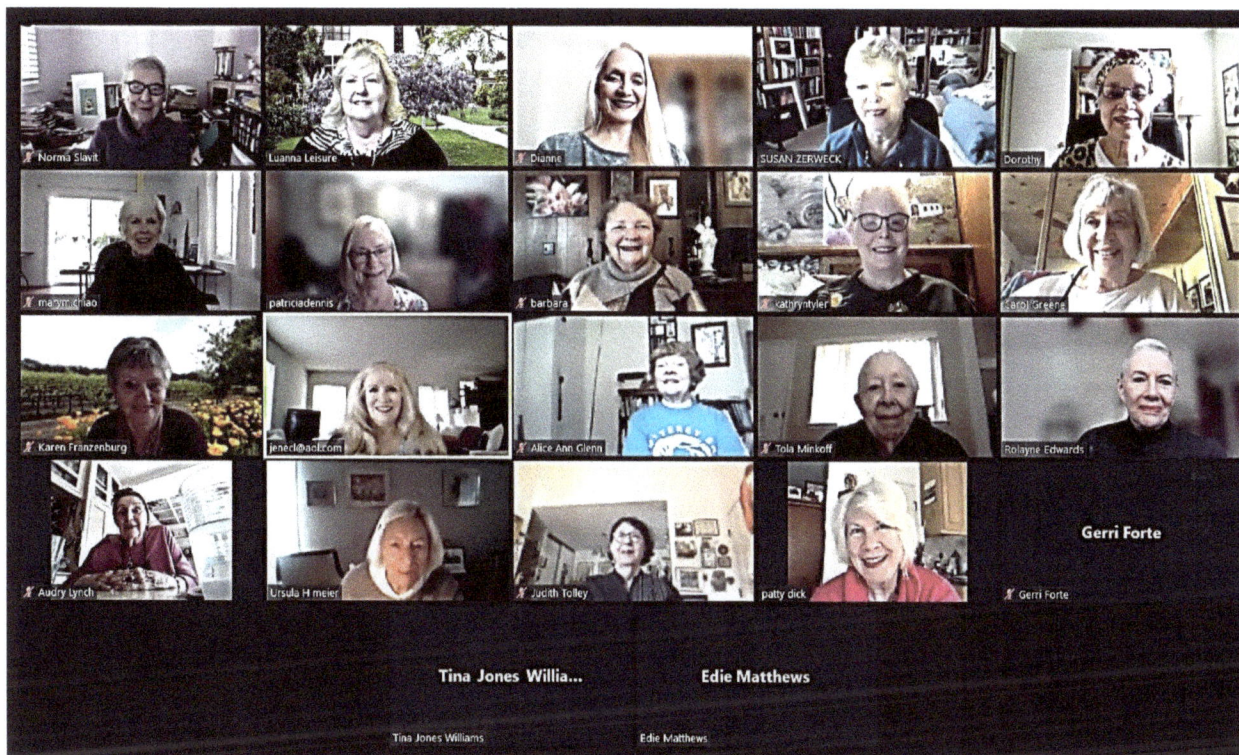

Special Guest Rolayne Edwards
Handwriting Analyst
November 6, 2021

Top down left to right:
Norma Slavit, Luanna Leisure, Dianne Glass MacNair, Susan Zerweck, Dorothy Atkins.
Mary Miller Chiao, Patricia Dennis, Barbara Chamberlain, Katy Tyler, Carol Greene.
Karen Franzenburg, Jeanne Carbone, Alice Ann Glenn, Tola Minkoff, Rolayne Edwards,
Audry Lynch, Ursula Meier, Judith Tolley, Patty Dick, Gerri Forté.
Tina Jones Williams, Edie Matthews.

Twenty Year Members
Congratulations

February 1, 2020 we started the tradition of honoring Pen Women who were members for 20 years or more. Covid-19 hit, so in 2021 we could not meet in person to celebrate our ladies who became members back in 2001; but all were still honored with their certificates. There were no new members in 2002.

Twenty Year Plus Members
Left to Right

Luanna K. Leisure, President
Dorothy Atkins, NorCal President
Evelyn Wofford, National President, Letters, 33 Year Member
Barbara Chamberlain, Letters 46 Year Life Member
ShaRon Haugen, Art, 28 Year Member
Ursula Meier, Letters, 25 Year Member
Tola Minkoff, Art, 21 Year Member
Alice Ann Glenn, Letters, 38 Year Member
Louise Webb, Letters, 28 Year Member
Audry Lynch, Letters, 25 Year Member
Carol Greene, Letters and Music, 20 Year Member
Susan Zerweck, Music, 29 Year Member
Patricia Dennis, Vice President
Patricia Suggs, Art 33 Year Member (not in photo)
Geraldine "Jerri" Scaife, 20 Year Art Member (not in photo)

Twenty Year Members
Congratulations

Celebrating and honoring our Pen Women who joined in 2001

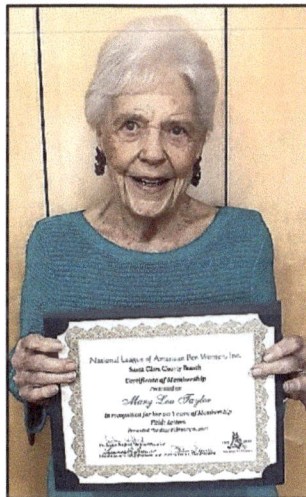

Twenty Year Members
Left to Right Start at the Top

Edie Matthews, Letters
Carol Brolin, Art
Bonnie Vaughan, Letters
Mary Lou Taylor, Letters
Dianne Glass MacNair, Letters

Christmas Together

**We Do Enjoy Being Together
Christmas Celebrations**

Home of Susan and Ralph Zerweck
2017

Left to right: Carol Greene, Tola Minkoff, Kathryn Tyler, Edie Matthews, Marcia Sivek, Pat Fisher, Diana Chan, ShaRon Haugen Patricia Dennis, Dorothy Brown, Carolina Mueller, Dorothy Atkins, Carol Brolin, Luanna Leisure.
Front: Susan Zerweck, Judith Shernock, Nancy Bloomer Deussen, Annette Tan.

Christmas Together

Home of Susan and Ralph Zerweck
2018

Back row: Carol Greene, Patricia Dennis, Pat Fisher, ShaRon Haugen, Claudia Gray, Marcia Sivek.
Second row: Dorothy Atkins, Jeanne Carbone, Jude Tolley.
Front row: Luanna Leisure, Barbara Chamberlain, Kathryn Tyler, Nancy Bloomer. Deussen, Lorna Kohler, Susan Zerweck.

Sing-a-long
and
Nancy would
play the
piano

Christmas Together

Fun to Have Fun
Carol Greene, Edie Matthews, Tola Minkoff, Susan Zerweck, Carolina Mueller,
Katy Tyler, ShaRon Haugen, Marcia Sivek

Christmas 2021
Before Omicron Virus Ravaged the U.S.
Left side: Kathryn Tyler, Louise Webb, Luanna Leisure, Rolayne Edwards, Elvira Rascov
Right side: Mary Miller Chiao, Patricia Dennis, Gail Lockhart, Karen Franzenburg, Patty Dick

Christmas Together

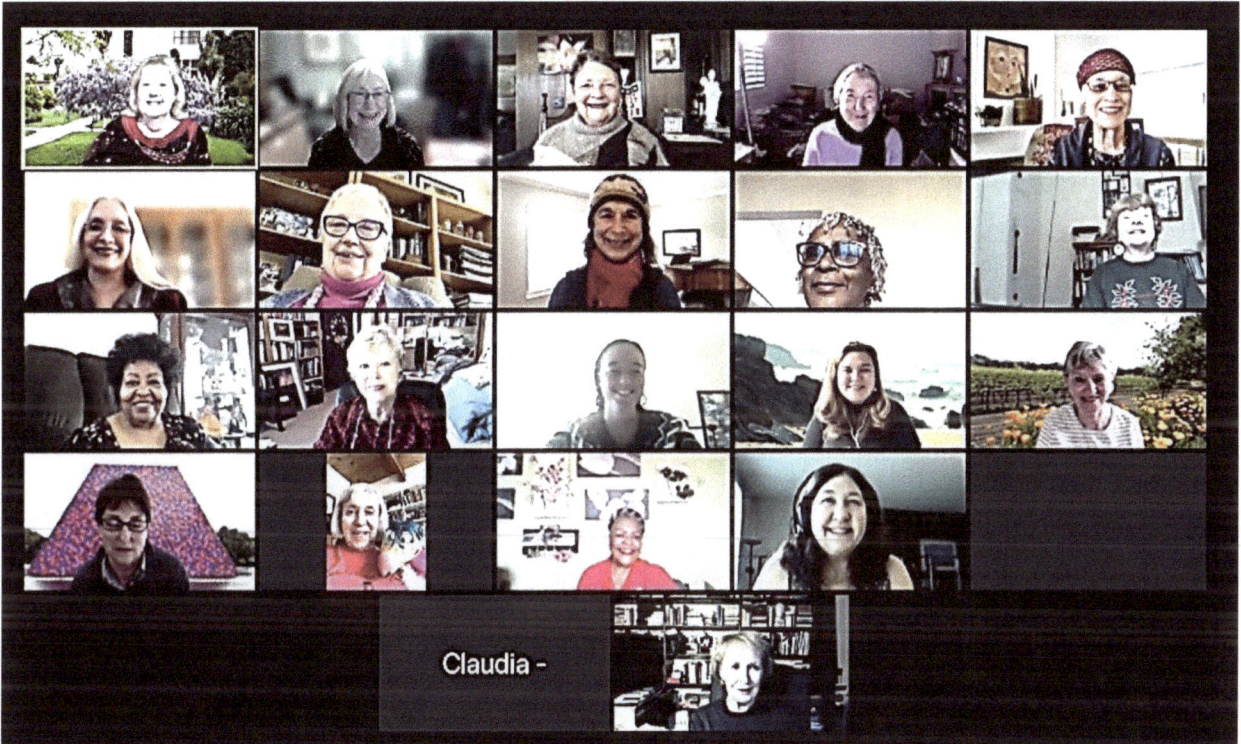

Zoom 2021 Christmas
Concerns about Omicron, so some of us zoomed

Left to right from top to bottom:
Luanna Leisure, Patricia Dennis, Barbara Chamberlain, Norma Slavit, Dorothy Atkins.
Dianne MacNair, Darlene Weingand, Lorna Kohler, Vanice Ellis, Alice Ann Glenn.
Gerrie Fortè, Susan Zerweck, Janie Oberhauser, Gevevieve Liu, Karen Franzenburg.
Bonnie Jo Smith. Carol Greene, Tina Jones Williams, Lorraine Gabbert.
Claudia Gray, Edie Matthews.

Celebrity Luncheons

Our Luncheons started in October 1922. The purpose evolved to honor professional women in the community who were talented in Music, Letters, and Art.

These women would receive a meal, a certificate, and an application for membership. They could also bring their artistic works to sell. The achievers were a main way of drawing in new members.

The luncheons were also our way to raise money for the scholarship awards for graduating high school seniors or college students who were talented in the arts and continuing their educations.

In December, members started gathering new and like new items to create the raffle baskets. Many would call and visit business owners in the community requesting donations. This was just the beginning.

The luncheons were an all day celebration which included performances, food, a basket raffle, and a silent auction.

ShaRon Haugen opened up her home for storage of these items. Then we would have a work party to create the lovely baskets and price the silent auction items.

It was a lot of work and lots of fun. Preparing for the Celebrity Luncheon took several months of preparation. Kudos to the all the women who continued this tradition over the years.

Because of Covid-19 we could not hold our luncheons. Our last luncheon was February 1, 2020. At that time we heard about a deadly pandemic that was spreading around the world. We didn't know that in a few short weeks our state would be in lockdown. And we also didn't realize that it would last two years going on three.

Instead of our scholarship fundraiser luncheons, Pen Women and donors from the community have mailed monetary donations to help keep our Scholarship Awards Program going.

Following are several pages of fond memories

Work Parties at
ShaRon Haugen's Home

It Takes Teamwork

Every Celebrity Luncheon Has a Theme

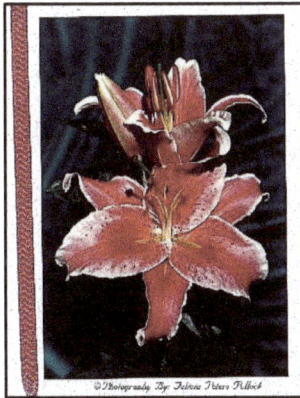

© Photography By: Felicia Peters Pollock

2000

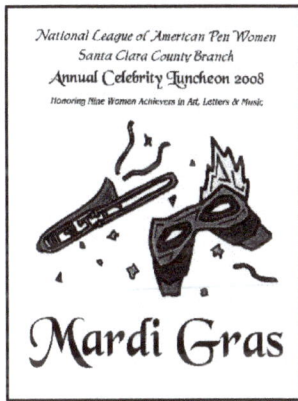

National League of American Pen Women
Santa Clara County Branch
Annual Celebrity Luncheon 2008
Honoring Nine Women Achievers in Art, Letters & Music

Mardi Gras

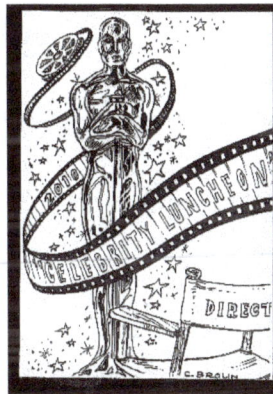

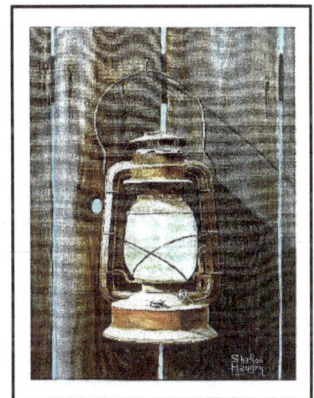

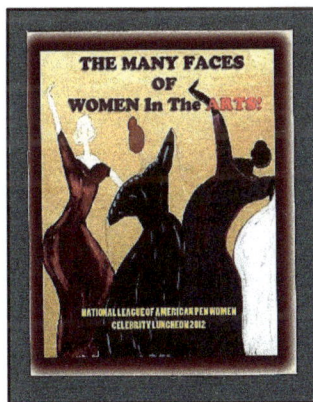

THE MANY FACES OF WOMEN In The ARTS!

NATIONAL LEAGUE OF AMERICAN PEN WOMEN
CELEBRITY LUNCHEON 2012

Venetian Carnivale

The National League of American Pen Women
Celebrity Luncheon 2014

The National League of American Pen Women
Celebrity Luncheon 2015

Celebrity Aloha 2016

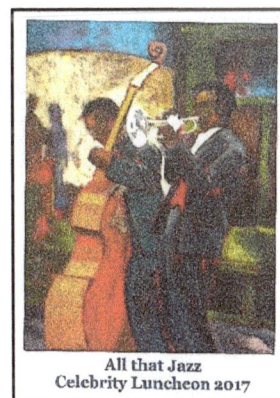

All that Jazz
Celebrity Luncheon 2017

Every Celebrity Luncheon Has a Theme

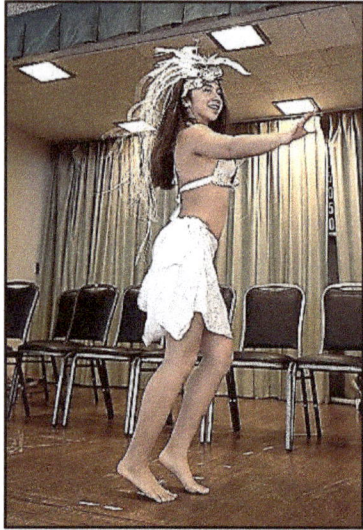

Juliana Monela

Carol Greene and
Reginald

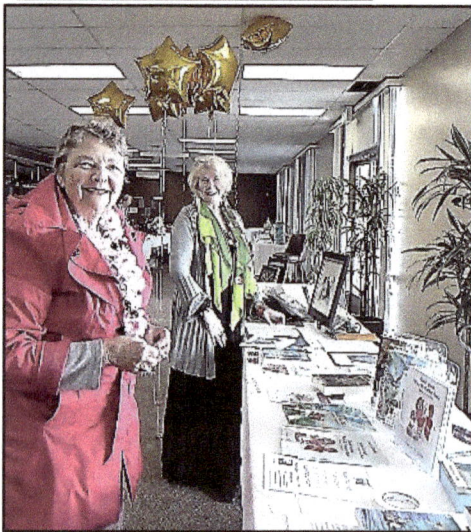

Pen Women Table
Barbara Chamberlain
and Patty Dick.

Alice Ann Glenn
and Dianne Glass MacNair

Every Celebrity Luncheon Happens Because of Volunteers

Susan Zerweck and
ShaRon Haugen

Edie Matthews and
Nancy Bloomer Deussen

2020 Achiever
Khalilah Ramirez

Selling Raffle Tickets

Left: Kay Duffy
Right: Carol Brolin

Wanting to Win the Raffle
Norma Slavit and
Paul Staschower
Bottom Left
Dianne Glass MacNair
Jeanne Carbone

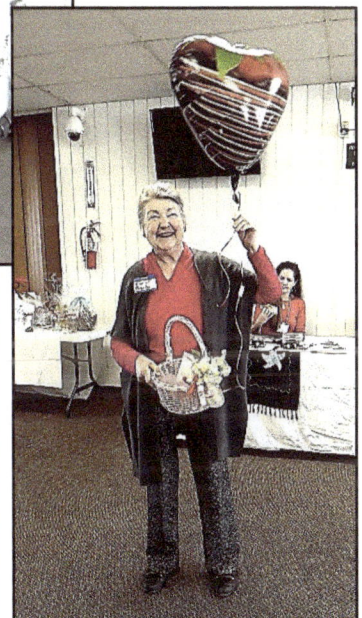

Raising Scholarship Funds – One Main Reason
for the Luncheons

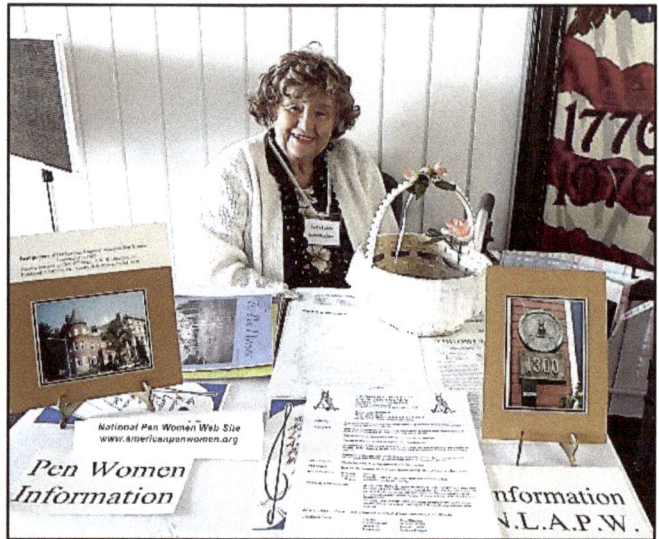

Information Table
Audry Lynch

Entertainment
Judy Bingman and
Nancy Bloomer Deussen

Nancy Bloomer Deussen on the piano
Mary Lou Taylor selling raffle tickets

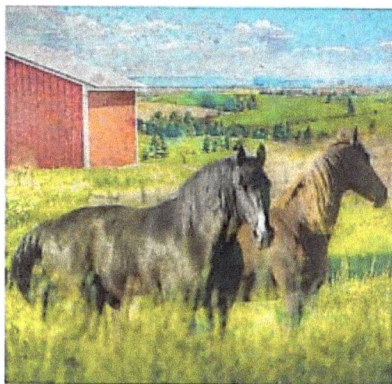

Make Mine Country Style

Celebrity Luncheon 2018

Behind the Scenes

Entertainment
Top Right Photo
Left to right:
Cyra Cowan, Susan Zerweck, Jeff Rippin, Melissa Conaulty, Len Anderson and Edie Matthews.

The Worker Bees
They Make it Happen!
Seated at the table:
Carolina Mueller, ShaRon Haugen, Pat Fisher, Patty and Lou Dick.

Back:
Alice Ann Glenn, Patricia Dennis, Cyra Cowan, Karen Franzenburg, Katy Tyler, Luanna Leisure, Marcia Sivek, Susan and Ralph Zerweck

National League of American Pen Women
Santa Clara County Branch

Celebrity Luncheon

February 2, 2019

A Bit of Auld Ireland

Irish Lassies
Patricia Dennis, Katy Tyler, Patty Dick

The Head Table Preparations
Susan Zerweck, Judy Bingman, Luanna Leisure,
National President, Evelyn Wofford, Patricia
Dennis and Dorothy Atkins

Keltic Katz
Helen Grange, Richard Katz, Luanna
Leisure, Linda Menard.

A Full House

National League of American Pen Women

Celebrity Luncheon

February 1, 2020

Pen Women Rock

Enjoyment Before Covid

We did not know our 2020 Celebrity Luncheon would be the last before Covid-19 hit. The night before our luncheon, we enjoyed a fine meal at Chef Chu's with National President, Evelyn Wofford then dessert at Diana Chan's. A few days later there was an excursion to Filoli Gardens organized by Patricia Dennis. We look back and appreciate the good times.

CHEF CHU's RESTAURANT
JANUARY 31, 2020

Chef Chu with Susan Zerweck and our National President, Evelyn Wofford

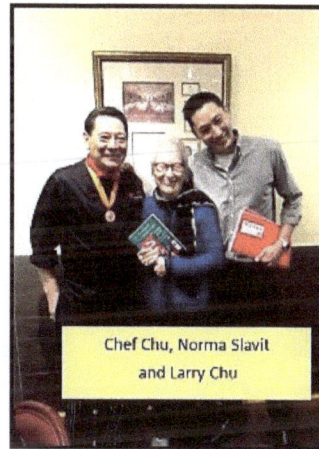

Chef Chu, Norma Slavit and Larry Chu

Left to right:
Susan Zerweck,
Chef Chu,
National Pres.,
Evelyn Wofford.
Chef Chu,
Norma Slavit,
Larry Chu.
Louise Webb,
Carol Greene,
Louise Webb,
Dorothy Atkins,
Susan Zerweck,
Evelyn Wofford,
Norma Slavit,
Patricia Dennis,
ShaRon Haugen,
Cyra Cowan.
Sharon Haugen,
Patricia Dennis,
Cyra Cowan.
Ursula Meier,
Patty Dick,
Audry Lynch.
Tola Minkoff,
Carol Brolin.

CHEF CHU's RESTAURANT

Left to right: Louise Webb, Susan Zerweck, Evelyn Wofford, Diana Chan, Karen Franzenburg, Carol Greene, Chef Chu, Norma Slavit, Luanna Leisure, Larry Chu, Dorothy Atkins, Carol Greene, Louise Webb, Dorothy Atkins, Susan Zerweck, Evelyn Wofford, Norma Slavit, Luanna Leisure, ShaRon Haugen, Cyra Cowan, Patricia Dennis.

DESSERT WITH DIANA CHAN

Left to right: Carol Brolin, Norma Slavit, Ursula Meier, Evelyn Wofford, Diana Chan, Susan Zerweck, Carol Greene, Diana Chan, Norma Slavit, Dorothy Atkins, Carol Brolin, Karen Franzenburg, Evelyn Wofford, Katy Tyler, Ursula Meier, Cyra Cowan, Louise Webb, ShaRon Haugen, Susan Zerweck, Patty Dick, Tola Minkoff, Patricia Dennis.

FILOLI GARDENS
FEBRUARY 3, 2020

Fun at Filoli's

Top photo left to right: Dorothy Atkins, Luanna Leisure, Lori Howell Thompson, Patricia Dennis, Kay Duffy, Susan Zerweck, Evelyn Wofford.

Achievers
Just a few Achievers from over the years

1976 Achievers

THE PEN—ARTS BUILDING

The Pen-Arts Building, within walking distance of fashionable Connecticut Avenue and not too far from the White House itself, is the scene of gracious Pen Women receptions. The glittering chandeliers in drawing room and dining room, and the nine fireplaces each with its original mantel provide an air of dignity.

The Santa Clara County Branch of the National League of American Pen Women, Inc., proudly announce their annual list of achievers in Art and Letters, this fourteenth day of February, nineteen hundred and seventy-six, at San Jose, California.

Speakers: Eldon Dedini, Cartoonist, and Artist, Marjorie Close

ARTISTS:	WRITERS:
Sandra Craft	Joan Coombs
Wanda Faust	DAryle Seil
Marian Ferri	Mary Gerbino
Esther Grove	Virginia Golden
Ted Maddock	Anita Goldwasser
Bette Paris	Beverly Hammel
Edward Ramirez	Esther Herr
Jean Sarensen	Mary Lou Lyon
Stanley Wacholz	Patricia Pfeiffer
	Esther Talbot

Photographer and Writer
Professor S.I. Fisher

Madge Saksena, President
Charlotte Dunn, Achiever Chairman,
Phyllis McCallum, Chairman of Celebrity
Jacqueline Cathcart, M.C..

Achievers
Just a few Celebrities from over the years

Dorothy Atkins
2007 Achiever
Surprise meet with high school classmate, **Judy Bingman** who was an achiever in **2004**

2014 Achievers
Brenda Elliott, Carla Almanza-deQuant, Susan Taylor Brown, Jo Cooley, Luanna Leisure, Maria Grusauskas, Teresa Orozco, Marilyn August

2015 Achievers

Carolyn Larsen
Patricia Sherwood
Ann Bridges
Claire Mullin
Marie Cameron
Deanna Grenier-Mullins
Melody Sheppard
Patricia Dennis

2016 Achievers

Norma Slavit
Marjorie Johnson
Ushma Vahia
Christine Van Hoy
June Laman
Giselle Gatreau
Jeanne Tillman
Mary Ann Savage
Photo by Patricia
Dennis

The National League Of American Pen Women
Santa Clara Branch
2016 Achievers

Lijah Roof   Diana Chan   Bonnie Jo Smith   Erica Goss   Julia Watson   Lille Mcghee Queen   Cymber Lily Quinn   Dorothy Brown

2017 Achievers

Lijah Raoof
Diana F. Chan
Bonnie Jo Smith
Erica Goss
Julia Watson
Lilli McGhee Queen
Cymber Lily Quinn
Dorothy Brown
Photo by Patricia Dennis

2018 Santa Clara County Branch of the National League of American Pen Women
Achievers

2018 Achievers

Susan Zerweck, Chair
Tina Jones Williams
Annette Tan
Marcia Sivek
Judith Shernock
Pat Fisher
Lorna Kohler
Ruth Huber
Lorraine Lawson
Karen Franzenburg
Photo by Patricia Dennis

2019 Achievers
Anna Miakisk,
Alexandra
Beltran,
Claudia Gray
Jude Tolley
Elvira Rascov
Chair, Susan
Zerweck
Not in photo:
Barbara Tinsley
Photo by Patricia
Dennis

2020 Achievers

Left to right back row: Pen Women, Lorna Kohler and Jeanne Carbone. Achievers Khalilah Ramirez, Danielle Dufayet, Holly Van Hart, JoAnneh Nagler, Jade Bradley, Lisa Marino Becker, and Pen Woman, Susan Zerweck, Achiever Chair.
Front three ladies, Dani Burton, Harriett Arnold, Tracy Beardsley
Photo by Patricia Dennis

Tea at Edie's

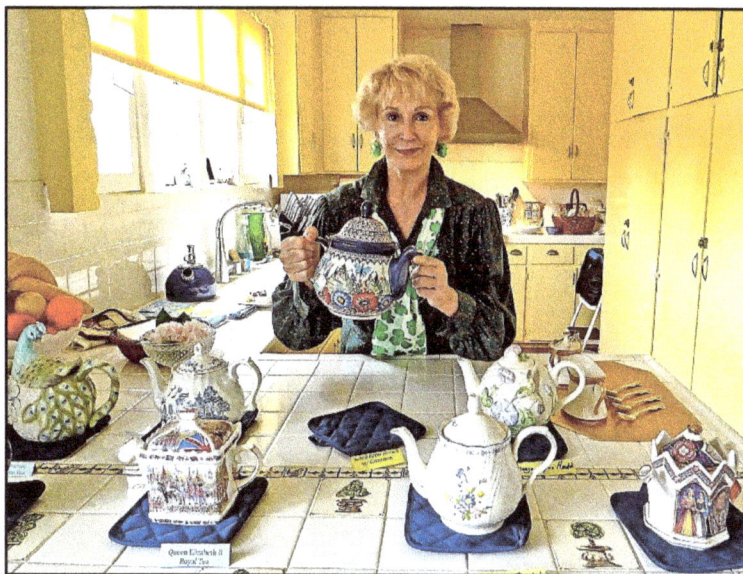

Annual Tea
at the home of Edie Matthews

In March Edie invites Pen Women, Achievers and New Members to a lovely and elegant tea party. This is a highlight we all look forward to each year. Because of the Pandemic we have been unable to enjoy Edie's tea but we are hoping for May 7, 2022. At this time we will honor our new members, scholarship recipients, and hand out our 100 Anniversary Commemorative Book.

Good Times
Good Food
Good Friends
Left to right: Brenda Elliott, Susan Zerweck, Edie Matthews, Carol Greene, Carol Brolin, Cleo McDowell, Nancy Bloomer Deussen, Mary Miller Chiao.

Photo next page top left: Mary Lou Taylor

Tea at Edie's
Beautiful Table and Delicious Tea

Community Outreach
Activities and Presentations

Carol Brolin, Illustrator
Luanna Leisure, Author
NLAPW Outreach Workshop
August 20, 2017

First Grade Class at Marshall Lane Elementary
Priscilla Spencer, Principal
Denise Yang, First Grade Teacher

The workshop taught the students the difference between being an author and an illustrator. The students had a week to pair up by twos. One would write the story and the other would draw the illustrations to go along with the story. They stapled their books on the edges then each pair took turns reading their stories. Permission was granted by the parents of the children to use photographs for publicity. Photos by Judy Bingman

Author and Illustrator
Students learned about the ins and outs of creating a book.

The children's books were on display at the NLAPW 120th Anniversary at the Pen Arts Building in Washington, D. C.

San Jose Women's Club and NLAPW

Dorothy Atkins, Outreach Chair
April 28, 2015
Presentation at San Jose Women's Club
on Madam C. J. Walker
First Black Millionaire in the United States

Dorothy brought her mother-in-law, Roberta Atkins'
hats. Pen Women love hats.
Photos by Luanna Leisure

Pen Women
Left to right: Patty Dick, Susan Zerweck, Brenda
Elliott, Audry Lynch

Louise Webb
Prize purchase. Once the
owner of over 300 hats.

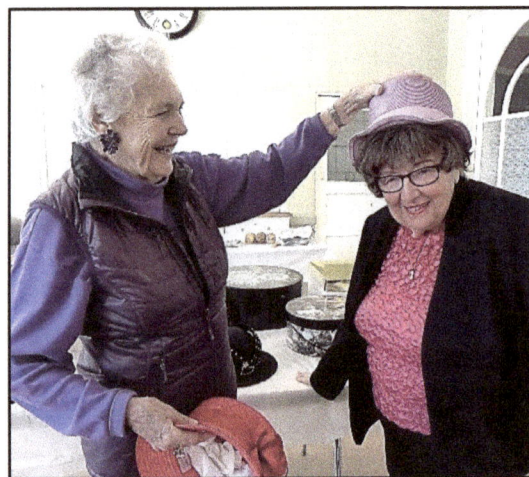

Mary Lou Taylor and Audry Lynch
Fun trying on hats

58

San Jose Women's Club and NLAPW Chamber Music

An Afternoon of Chamber Music

April 17, 2016

Featuring the Compositions of Nancy Bloomer Deussen
Performed by the Messiah Brass
San Jose Women's Club and Pen Women Event
Also – Pen Women – Authors' Book Fair

Left to right: MC and Pen Woman, Edie Matthews, Composer and Pen Woman, Nancy Bloomer Deussen, Messiah Brass.

San Jose Women's Club and NLAPW Book Fair

Pen Women – Authors' Book Fair
San Jose Women's Club and Pen Women Event
April 17, 2016
Left to right: Composer, Nancy Bloomer Deussen, Bonnie Vaughan, Barbara Chamberlain, Kathryn Tyler, Marjorie Johnson, Patty Watkins Dick, Mary Lou Taylor, Audry Lynch.

San Jose Women's Club and NLAPW
We are Pen Women

We are Pen Women
September 25, 2017

Introducing Pen Women to the San Jose Women's Club, arranged by Dorothy Atkins. Because of this outreach, our SCC Branch now shares networking and membership opportunities with the San Jose Women's Club.

Left to right: Nancy Bloomer Deussen, Patricia Dennis, Carol Brolin, Luanna Leisure, Dorothy Atkins.

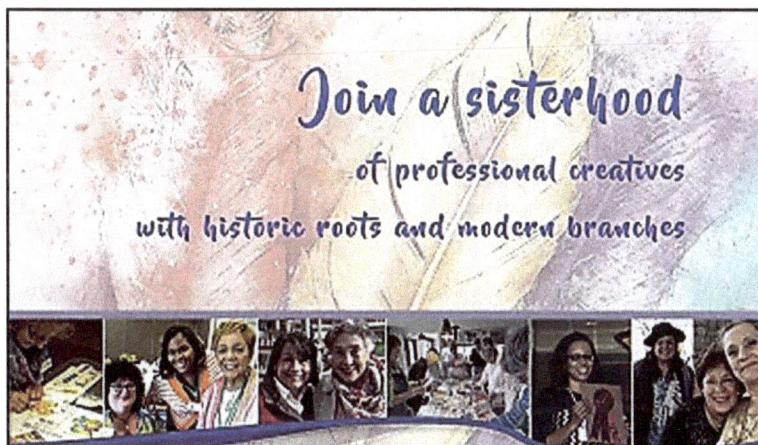

Join a sisterhood
of professional creatives
with historic roots and modern branches

San Jose Women's Club and NLAPW Zoom Presentations

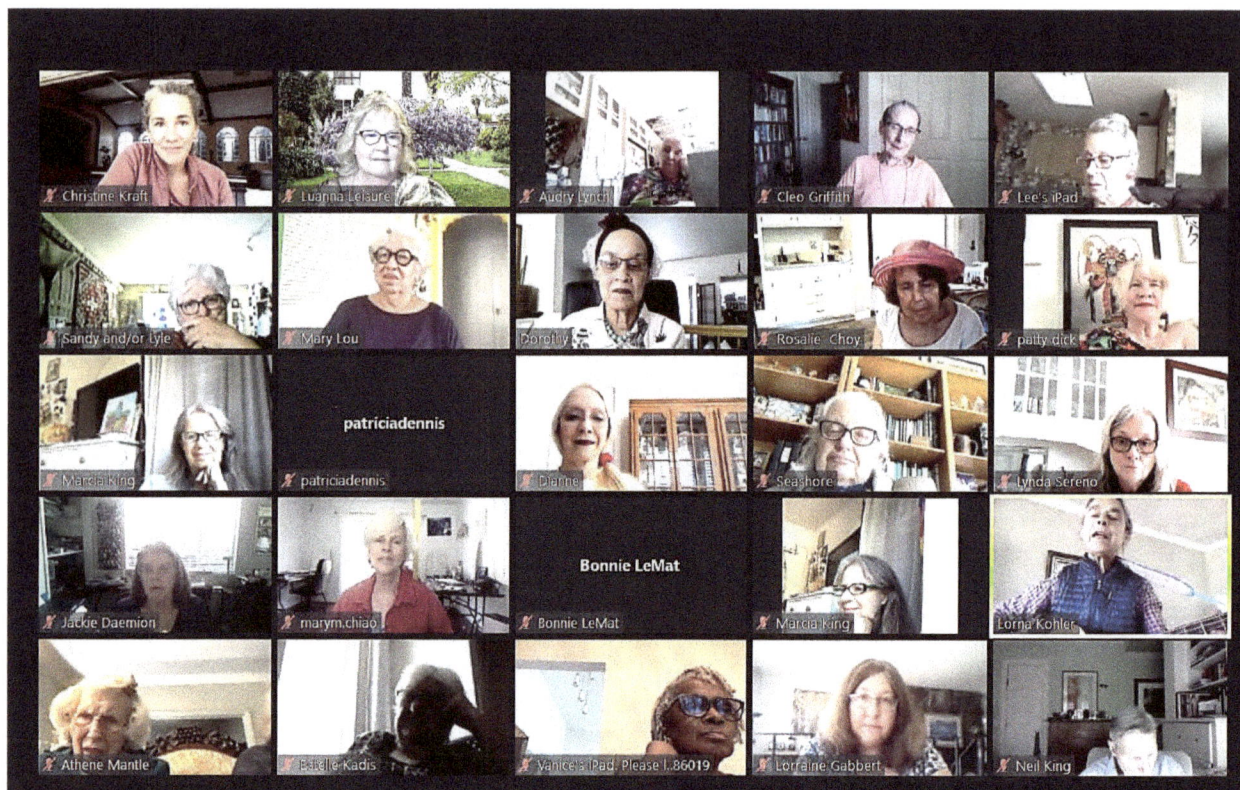

Introduction to Pen Women
Hosted by San Jose Women's Club
September 20, 2021

The San Jose Women's Club has invited the Santa Clara County Branch three times since the pandemic started to make presentations. One presentation featured Dorothy Atkins giving a talk on Social Unrest from the point of view of a woman of color. Another presentation featured Louise Webb who discussed her career interviewing famous celebrities.

The above screenshot presentation featured several Pen Women in a Show and Tell to introduce themselves to the SJ Women's Club. The Women's Club offered free membership to Pen Women.

Left to right top down: Christine Kraft, Luanna Leisure, Audry Lynch, Cleo Griffin, Lee, Sandy Swairsky, Mary Lou Mason, Dorothy Atkins, Louise Webb, Patty Dick, Marcia King, Patricia Dennis, Dianne MacNair, Darlene Weingand, Linda Sereno, Jacie Daemion, Mary Miller Chiao, Bonnie LeMat, Marcia King, Lorna Kohler, Athene Mantle, Estelle Kadis, Vanice Ellis, Lorraine Gabbert, Neil King.

Outreach - Networking
Pen Women, Saratoga Senior Center, and Louise Webb's Memoirs Class

Louise Webb's Memoirs Class
Including six Pen Women

Pen Woman, Louise Webb, has taught her class at the Saratoga Senior Center for over 22 years. Over the years many Pen Women have been a part of her class, and many of the members of her class are friends and supporters of Pen Women, attending our Celebrity Luncheons and activities.
Back row: Executive Assistant SASCC, Raj, Kauri, John Kimball, Diana Chan, Grace Bush, John Poole, Dorothy Atkins, Judy Bingman, Chuck Chaffin, Minda Schwartz
Front row: Jing-Shi Su, Luanna Leisure, Dorothy Clapp, Norma Slavit, Patricia Dennis, Louise Webb, Debby Freeman, Rolayne Edwards, Joan Gomersall.
Louise Webb's class is still meeting on zoom.

Outreach - Networking
Tyler Taylor Director of SASCC

Outreach and Networking at its Best
April 14, 2018
Pen Women, Louise Webb's Memoirs Class and Tyler Taylor,
Saratoga Senior Center, all working together

Tyler Taylor, Executive Director of the Saratoga Area Senior Coordinating Council (SASCC) donated a $1,500 scholarship in honor of Louse Webb and her Memoirs Class to a student through our SCC Branch Scholarship Awards program.

Left to right: Dianne Glass MacNair, Patricia Dennis, Dorothy Atkins, Louise Webb, Luanna Leisure, Tyler Taylor, Chuck Chaffin, Jing-Shi Su, Debbie Freeman. Front and center: Scholarship Recipient, Micaela Daney.

NLAPW

Santa Clara Co. Branch

Community Outreach
Saratoga Senior Center — May 3, 2019

Dorothy Atkins, our Community Outreach Chair, organized an event at a luncheon located at the Saratoga Senior Center on May 3rd.

Our "Why I am a Pen Woman" outreach video was played as an introduction. Then Dorothy talked about our branch and introduced member, Lorna Kohler, who entertained with her lovely singing. Dorothy then introduced Luanna Leisure who talked about our celebrity luncheon and scholarship awards program. Luanna also introduced Louise Webb as a Pen Woman and as the leader of her Memoirs Class there at the senior center. Luanna introduced Patricia Dennis who ran a video of her beautiful photography.

Several pen women came and supported the event. Pat Fisher, ShaRon Haugen, Mary Lou Taylor, Audry Lynch, Louise Webb and Katie Tyler.

Sock Drive

Sock Drive for Those Without
November 2019

The Saratoga Senior Center, Louise Webb's Memoirs Class and the Santa Clara County Pen Women jointly worked together to provide warm socks for those in need.

Back row: Luanna Leisure, ShaRon Haugen. **Middle row:** Tina Jones Williams, Patricia Dennis, Nancy Bloomer Deussen, Jude Tolley, Ursula Meier, Pat Fisher. **Front row:** Tola Minkoff, Norma Slavit, Dorothy Atkins, Karen Franzenburg, Alice Ann Glenn, Patty Watkins Dick.

Socks Delivered

Luanna Leisure, Dorothy Atkins and Patricia Dennis delivered socks to the Foothill Community Presbyterian Church who distributed the socks to shelters.

The combined efforts of the memoirs class, Saratoga Senior Center, and the Pen Women netted well over 600 pairs of socks.

Coastal Arts League
September 1, 2018

Art Show at Coastal Arts League
Half Moon Bay
Top left photo back: Pat Fisher, Luanna Leisure, Marcia Sivek, Dorothy Atkins.
Front: Patricia Dennis, ShaRon Haugen

Campbell Artist's Guild

Pen Women Win!

August 3, 2019

Jude Tolley, Best of Show

Karen Franzenburg

Patricia Dennis

Claudia Gray

Virtual Art Show

2020
Congrats to the winners of our Virtual Art Show. Dorothy Atkins, Elvira Rascov and Karen Franzenburg
View the Art Show at www.nlapwsantaclara.org
Patricia Dennis Curator

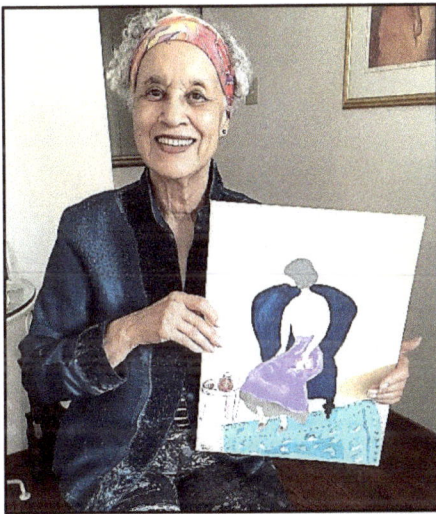

Dorothy Atkins
Most Public Votes

Dorothy Atkins
First Place

Elvira Rascov
2nd Place

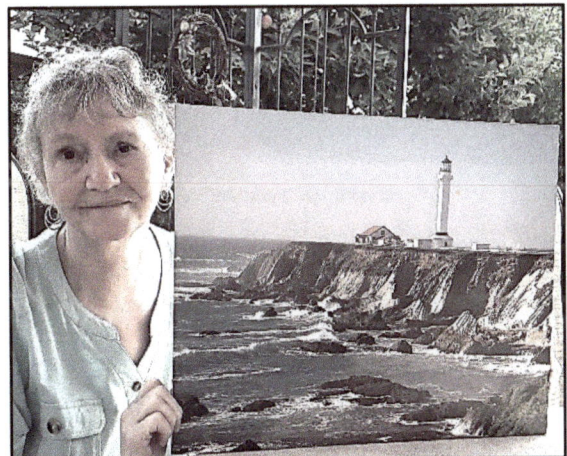

Karen Franzenburg
3rd Place

Author's Showcase Series

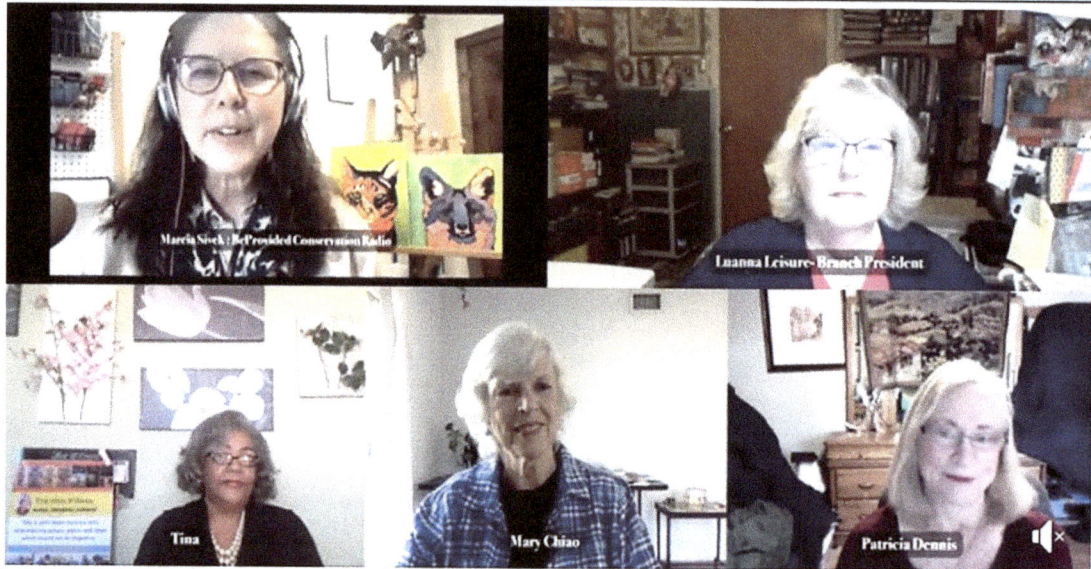

Marcia Sivek
Hosted Author Showcase

The pandemic made it impossible to hold meetings and presentations in public. Branch Secretary and Pod Caster, Marcia Sivek, made it happen virtually.

Live Facebook interviews with Santa Clara County Branch Authors as they discussed their books.

Top to bottom: Marcia Sivek, Luanna Leisure: Ledra's Book, Tina Jones Williams: A Delicate Balance, Mary Miller Chiao: Death on a Funeral Yacht A 1950's San Francisco Mystery, Patricia Dennis: Chasing a Pink Cadillac.

Below Part Two in Author Showcase Series

Dorothy Atkins: A Heady Scent of Lilac, Ariel Smart: Green Lantern and Other Stories, Barbara Chamberlain: The Jaden Steele Mysteries.

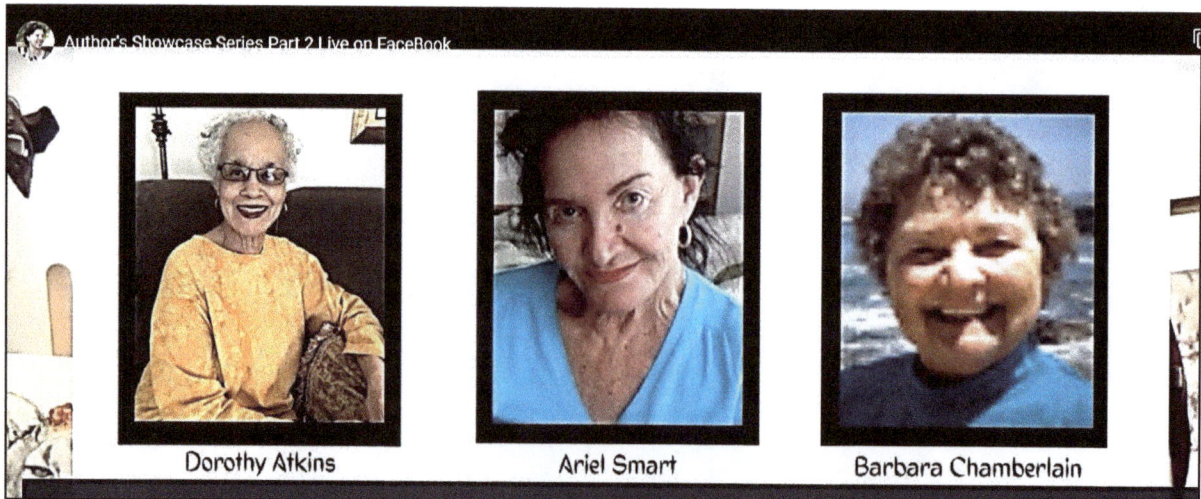

Dorothy Atkins   Ariel Smart   Barbara Chamberlain

Scholarship Awards
A Few Scholarship Recipients

The amounts have varied over the years, but the Santa Clara County Branch has continued to provide monetary awards for female high school senior students, undergraduate college students, or returning college students of any age who are talented in Art, Letters or Music.

Because of the pandemic we did not hold our celebrity luncheon in 2021 or 2022. This was our means of raising the funds for our awards. Instead we sent a letter to our donors and members who provided donations.

This year, in 2022, we are awarding three $1,000 awards. Because of Covid we are not sure if it will be safe enough to present the awards in person. It is our hope.

Scholarship Awards
June 5, 1999

Back Row Pen Women: Susan Zerweck, Erna Holyer, Beatrice Warren, Dale Lee, Dorothy Goble, Vallie Chan, Philomena Duran, Pat Eaager, ShaRon Haugen, Andria Dorrey, Norma Voth, Eloise Kirther, Fellicia Pollock.
Front Row Scholarship Recipients: Hlica Prioste, Lady Diane Decena, Lori Jensen, Tina Catania, Sharah Mayes, Michaela Rodriguez, Beth DiLeio, Kellie Lueder

A Few Scholarship Recipients

April 4, 2015 Winners
Jenny Duong
Catherine Pugh
Katelynn Walke
Genevieve Eckel
Micach Sinclair

April 1, 2017 Winners
Rachel Hildebrand
Elena Jorgenson
Isabella Baynard
Jeanna Sheen

April 6, 2019 Winners
Julia Torokhova
Ana Mata
Katie Watts
Raven Vujevich

Guess Who!
Guess who is behind the mask
Names Revealed on Page 134
No need to guess with our new name badge

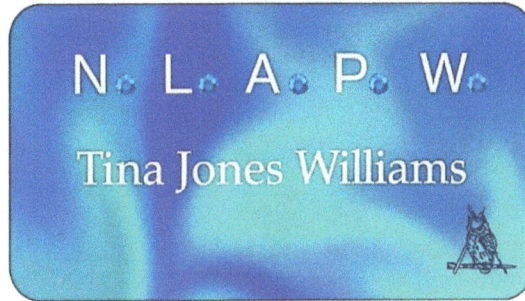

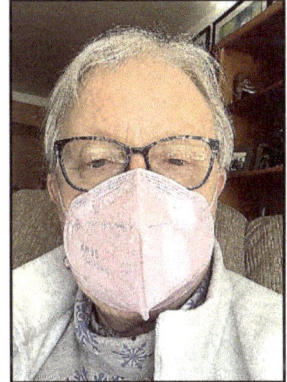

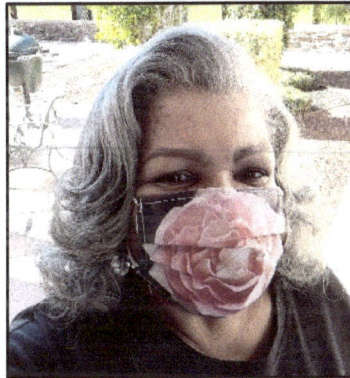

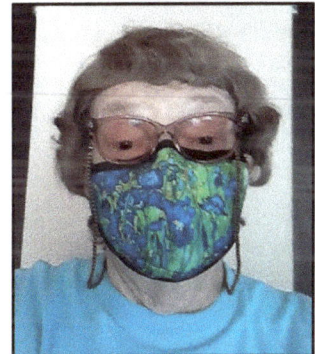

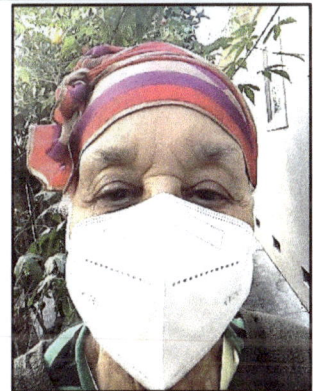

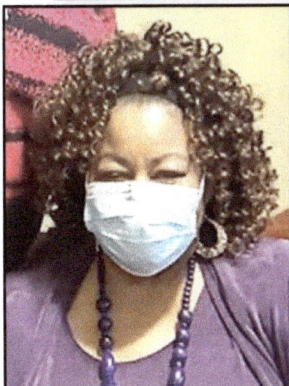

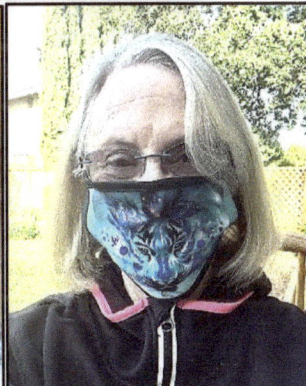

N . L . A . P . W .

Tina Jones Williams

Guess Who!

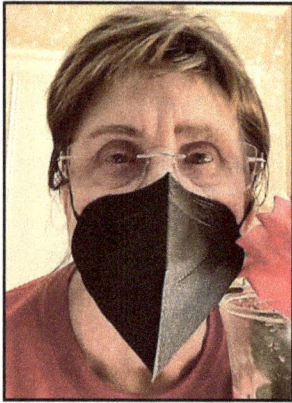
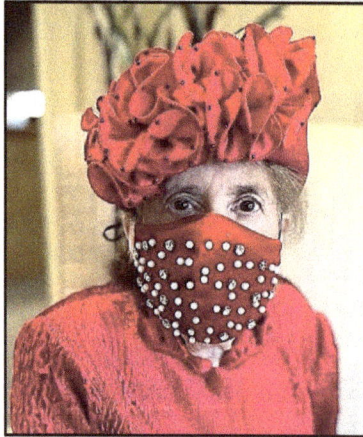
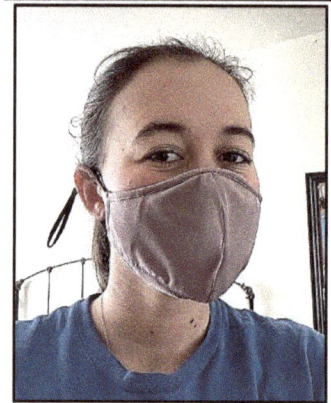
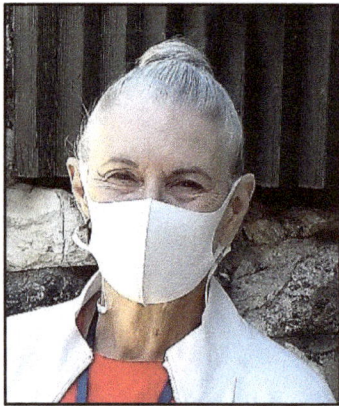
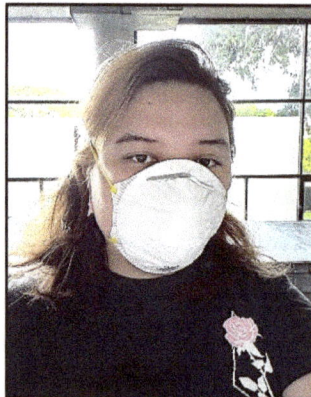

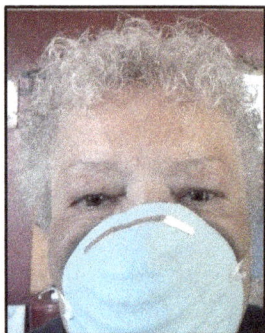
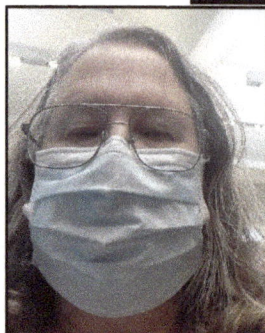

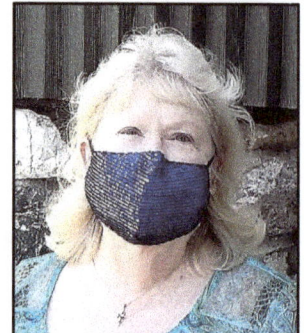

We Are Pen Women

Harriett Brown Arnold
Letters Member since 2017

It was during the spring of 2017 that an invitation to an Open Arts Studio Reception by a neighbor (Gloria Brown) provided me with an initial opportunity to be introduced to the National League of American Pen Women, specifically, the Santa Clara County Branch. In attendance were members Pat Fisher and Dorothy Atkins who shared the work of the Pen Women with me.

It was after the reception and our conversations that I began to investigate the organization. The mission and core values of respect, knowledge, creation, and preservation of the arts appealed to me for future membership.

The transition from academia has been different. My previous publications had been journal articles, textbooks, and educational professional books and articles. As I had been interested in exploring different forms of writing that were new to me, it was these three women who encouraged me to begin to think and take advantage of the friendship opportunities within the group.

Today, as a member of the branch, there are opportunities for me to network with like-minded women, women with similar professional interests, and to receive assistance in my continuous personal journey of discovery.

I am presently Professor Emerita in Benerd College, University of the Pacific, Stockton, California. I am a veteran educator and have served as an elementary school teacher, elementary school principal, international consultant, and director of personnel and staff development. I have served as a coordinator of the Stanford Teacher Education Program (STEP), Stanford University, Stanford, California.

My teacher training projects have involved teacher professional development for the Ministry of Education in the Bahamas, where I trained teachers in the area of reading, and in Japan, England, Trinidad, St. Maarten, Germany, Curacao, and Argentina in the area of social and emotional learning. Professionally, I continue to serve on the Executive Council of the Council of Accreditation for Educator Preparation (CAEP). This is the accrediting body for colleges and universities throughout the United States.

My publications include professional journal articles in early childhood education, teacher education, book reviews, one historical book, and four academic textbooks. Currently, my community service projects take place in Santa Clara County with an historic focus that include the Past President, San Jose State University Alumni Association, and the City of San Jose Historic Landmarks Commission.

As a member of the Santa Clara County Branch of the National League of American Pen Women (NLAPW), I continue my writing and publications. My current goal is to discover "what I want to be when I grow up." I also wish to grow old gracefully and to be filled with all the joys that life has ahead!

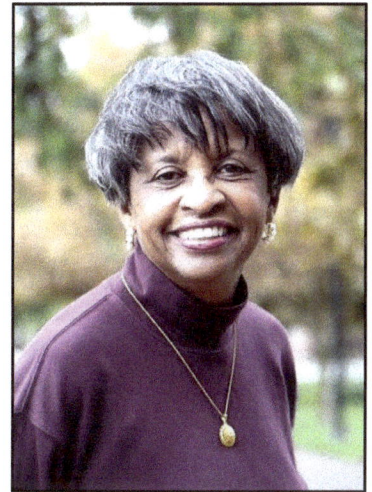

Dorothy Atkins
Art Member Since 2006

Being a Pen Women introduced me into a world of creative women who supported my work and my dreams. I am passionate about showing the world what we can achieve. I am proud to be a Pen Women as I see how collectively women can be a force in bringing professional talent forward. We are an inclusive organization that promotes other women and this is why I am honored to be a Pen Women.

My work is subtle, rhythmic, colorful, and poetic. I live my life with purpose as a highly energetic motivational speaker and entrepreneur with a line of greeting cards that once caught the eye of Robert Redford. My life was just beginning after many years in banking. Forecasting and number crunching left little time in my head to really make a serious attempt to do what I had longed to do for years: painting, writing poetry, and public speaking.

My acrylics and oils are vibrant in color and evoke the memories, wonder, and stories of my childhood and slices of my everyday life. The presence of women, soft, strong, joyful, and engaging take center stage in my work.

I am a self-taught artist maintaining humor, rhythm, and spirituality in my images, but I contend that art is a definite and continual sense of discovery.

During the lockdown and social unrest, my "One Love Series" was born. Each day I painted my feelings. Expressions of powerful women emerged. Consumed with the challenges of navigating a new normal, my canvas came alive with positive images. Each inspiration was purposefully painted to bring joy and healing.

I have exhibited my work at Gallery Saratoga, Bank of America, Guglielmo Winery, Saratoga Community Center, Saratoga Garden Art Show, La Quinta Hotel, MOAD (Museum of African Diaspora) San Francisco, Triton Museum, Los Gatos Jewish Community Center, Le Petit Trianon Theatre, Hayward Art Council, Half Moon Gallery, and the National League of American Pen Women Virtual Art Show.

My work has been featured in Charles Schwab Magazine and Internet Video, Scene Magazine, Victoria magazine, AARP, and various newspaper articles.

My paintings are in private collections throughout the world.

I am President of the Northern California National League of American Pen Women.

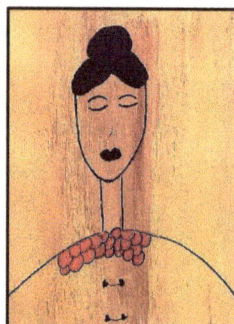

Marilyn August
Letters Member since 2015

In my professional life I was a virologist and laboratory scientist working in clinical laboratory medicine and biotechnology. Through the years as a scientist, I produced a bibliography of scientific papers, a textbook chapter, and presentations in academic settings as well as in the corporate environment. Having spent so much time writing in my career, after retirement I took on scientific writing and editing assignments. The major work was as co-author of a book on the history of diagnostic virology, *To Catch a Virus*, published in 2013 with John Booss.

My introduction to Pen Women was through member Maralyn Miller, whom I met when we were volunteers at the San Jose Museum of Art. After the book was published, I was honored by Maralyn's nomination in 2014 as an "Achiever in Letters," and she encouraged me to join the Santa Clara Branch of Pen Women. I appreciate being a member of an organization that promotes the development of the creative talents of women in the arts and that supports young people to pursue careers in the arts.

Although my career was in science, I was always interested in the arts. My sister, Bonnie August, was a well-known fashion designer in New York and created the "disco look" for Danskin, pairing leotards with wrap-around skirts and popularizing body wear as street wear. My father, in his 80's began his "art career, developing a unique style of pencil portraits of friends and neighbors. My mother was artistic in decorating and always stylish in her dress.

In college I spent a semester abroad in Florence, learned Italian, and studied art. I still speak and study Italian and have maintained close contact with my "Italian sister" and have visited her many times.

My undergraduate education was in microbiology at the University of Massachusetts at Amherst and doctoral studies at Columbia University. After post-doctoral training at Yale University School of Medicine, I accepted a position in Los Angeles and set up the diagnostic virology laboratory at Cedars-Sinai Medical Center, followed by positions at other large laboratories in Southern California.

After thirteen years, I took on the challenge of the biotechnology industry and moved to San Jose to join a start-up company devoted to viral vaccine development. There I contributed to the successful licensure in 2003 of FluMist®, a nasal spray vaccine for influenza.

Art and travel have always been my passions. My adventures have been mostly in Europe; however, I've made two trips to Africa, the most recent in May, 2019. I volunteered for 2 weeks at an animal sanctuary, N/a'ankusê, in Namibia. It was a fabulous experience—working hard, feeding and caring for the animals, and learning about the perils and conservation of wildlife in Namibia. I even had opportunities to be "up close and personal" with the baby baboons as shown in the photo.

Early on in the COVID-19 pandemic in 2020, I joined Art Yard BKLYN (artyardbklyn.org) for my first experience in an art class, which meets virtually each week on Zoom. Students comprise a diverse group of all ages and levels of expertise, including professional artists, most from around NYC and others scattered across the country. As a beginner, it's been an enriching and humbling experience, allowing me to join a community of new friends and to be challenged and supported in a safe, engaging environment.

Tracy Beardsley
Art Member since 2021

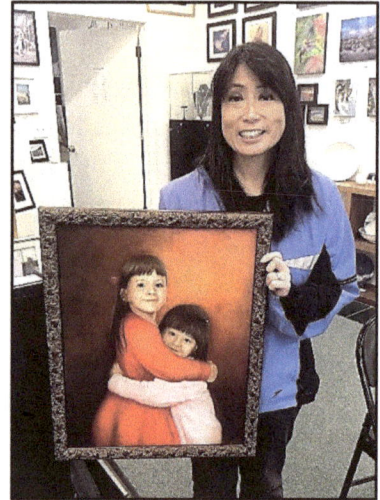

I am an artist and live on the San Mateo Coast. I love to paint the ocean, inspired by marine life in the area. Although I have a full-time job, a family, and a hectic life; I find painting exhilarating and enjoyable. It allows me to create a portal, peering into another world. I have participated in group shows at local libraries, San Mateo City Hall, and local art shows. I hope that the viewer will be reminded of the beauty and splendor of the ocean, and all of the great adventures yet to be had.

I also have teaching credentials for the craft of Kimekomi dolls. Kimekomi means "to tuck" and is an ancient art in Japan, using techniques to insert fabric into a wooden form. I participate and exhibit my dolls, along with the Mataro Doll Association (San Francisco East Bay Miyabi Mikai), every year at the San Francisco Cherry Blossom Festival and various other events in and around the Bay Area. I love the challenge that this craft requires, and it is an important part of my heritage and culture.

I met pen woman, Dorothy Atkins, at the Coastal Arts League, and she encouraged me to join the National League of American Pen Women. I love being a part of such a great group of talented, supportive, and gregarious women focusing on the creative arts and excellence.

Carol Brolin
Art Member since 2005

I love being a Pen Woman. I like the caliber of women: warm, intelligent, creative, and supportive of each other. We need that same frame of mind. The opportunities are there to work together, networking and expanding our own talents by learning from other Pen Women.

I have always been an artist, whether on stage in the theatre or rendering my talent on canvas with a brush or on paper with a pencil. When it came time to decide which path to take as a career, I realized that the path to acting schools and acceptance into the field could mean major compromises with my moral beliefs. I had heard the stories of women who had to sleep their way to success.

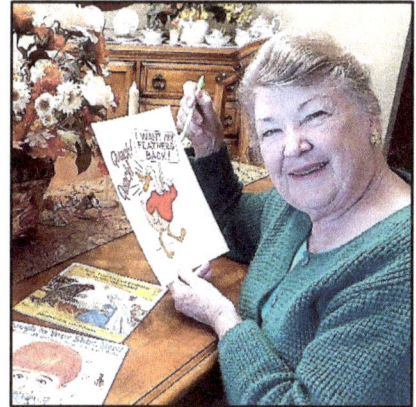

Creating illustrations, still life portraits, scenery, and landscapes won over as my true love in expressing my feelings and revealing my multitalented abilities. Inspired and encouraged by an aunt and uncle, I developed art skills early. I studied at Parson's School of Design in New York City. With my artistic ability, I readily found employment with department stores and businesses before computers took over the industry. It was a time when all ads were illustrated by hand, usually on a weekly basis. I illustrated ads for Liberty House in Hawaii, Mervyn's, Macy's, Long's Drug Store, and Steinbeck's in New Jersey, just to name a few. Computers drastically changed the industry. I was forced out of my career when a computer was placed on my desk and a graphic artist did the same work in less than half the time. This did not stop me. I went to work for Hewlett-Packard in the data entry department and later at HP's credit union. This was not a job in the arts, but I used my talents to create flyers and advertisements for the company and continued my work and studies in art.

I am still a professional illustrator and have continued being active and busy with my art. I didn't sit around and bemoan the fact that my career was yanked away; instead, I reinvented my style. I have collaborated with other Pen Women and illustrated five children's books written by three Pen Women: *Money. . . Cool*! by Judith Fabris, *A Very, Very Special Birthday* and *Cough in Your Shirt, Bert!* by Sheralee Hill Iglehart, and *Quack! Quack! I Want My Feathers Back*! by Luanna K. Leisure.

I have participated in numerous art workshops in locations around the world, including San Miguel de Allende in Mexico. I enrolled in a workshop on the Amalfi Coast in Italy and a workshop in Venice through Stanford University. I also taught fashion illustration at a community college. My art has been on display in different areas around the Santa Clara Valley. I am also a participant, along with other Pen Women, in the Outreach Program, which brings the world of art to the community and grade school students.

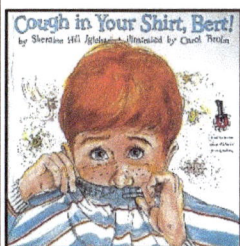

81

Jeanne C. Carbone
Art and Letters Member since 2003

I had never heard of the National League of American Pen Women until I took a class from one of its members.

Her name was Erna Holyer, and she taught Fact and Fiction for Fun and Profit for adult education for more than 30 years. She was responsible for instructing dozens of its members in Santa Clara County to become published authors and writers besides authoring 18 books herself.

I had read about Erna and her class for several years in the *Almaden Times*, a neighborhood newspaper in the early 2000s. I had always written, from my first short story at age 14, to poetry, to writing monologues for performances, to entering jokes for Reader's Digest. I wanted to take my writing to the next level and Erna, though I didn't know it at the time, was my answer to a new career. Within three years, under her tutelage, I was published in several magazines, had won first prize for the California Pioneers of Santa Clara County essay contest, reported local news for seven neighborhood newspapers under the *Times* masthead, and soon became the managing editor of all the papers. She also sponsored me to become a Pen Woman and a writing Achiever in Letters for the South Bay Branch where she was a member. Sadly, Erna died in 2007; and in a full circle moment, I wrote her obituary in the same Almaden Times newspaper where I had first read about her.

From the first place award in kindergarten for my crayon drawing of an elephant to the first short story I wrote in seventh grade, the arts have always been important to me. I studied both in college, and have taken classes from noted authors and painters throughout my life. I guess what I most desire in my creative process is to present what I'm feeling in the here and now. What thoughts, what feelings, in words or in visuals express who I truly am and what I feel today? Interspersed with world events and how they mold an individual's life are also represented in my work. How can they not be?

Besides writing, editing, and photography for the *Times Neighborhood Newspapers*, I have written for Ladies Home Journal (second place winner of the 2000 Power to Change essay), the Hellenic Voice, Industry and Salute magazines, The Spectator, among others. I was honored to be named the 2003 First Prize Award for the California Pioneers essay contest, 2004 National League of American Pen Women Achiever in Writing and subsequently in Art in 2008. The Silicon Valley Art Coalition Fete the Press was awarded to me in 2009. In the 2010's, along with my *Almaden* and *Evergreen Times* staff and publishers, we were awarded by both the San Jose City Council and the Santa Clara County Board of Supervisors Commendation Awards for our newspapers. Needless to say it was quite a thrill from my hometown! ***Personal mottos:*** *"Just do it!" and "Make it work"!*

Barbara Chamberlain
Letters Life Member since 1974

When I was about nine or ten, incidents that happened would make themselves into stories in my mind. Sometimes the stories were fantasy that came from my imagination. I started to write them down and even illustrated some of them. None of my classmates did this. The tendency to make up so many stories made me think I was different. I even started a school newspaper that I copied on an old mimeograph machine. Sometimes my teachers would ask me if I was copying my stories. That made me feel even more strange. Only when I started going to writing classes and seminars did I realize there were others like me.

I was selling short stories when a friend invited me to a Pen Women meeting. Our branch had a writers' workshop that I loved because it made me produce stories. The women in the workshop knew what constructive criticism was. They always had ideas of where a story might go, if a mistake had been made, or if there was a way to improve the text. One time a workshop member told me that the short story I had read sounded like the beginning of a novel. I really loved the writers' workshop.

The way Pen Women encourages others in the group and in meetings is certainly the reason I have written twelve novels and published six of them. Our branch president, Luanna Leisure, helped with self-publishing my last book, or I probably would have given up because the procedures had changed so much.

Pen Women is an outstanding example of encouraging women in the arts. I am so glad that my friend invited me to a Pen Women meeting long ago.

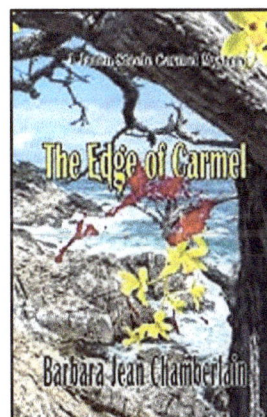

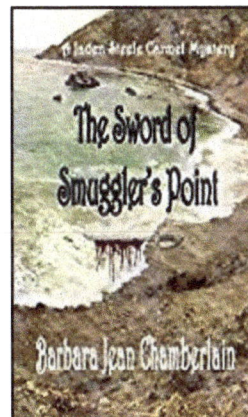

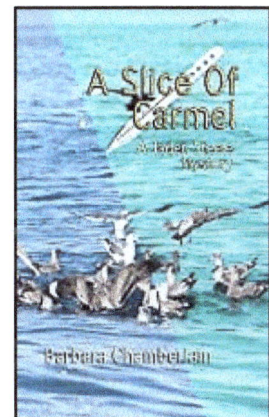

The Flight of Alpha 1
Barbara Chamberlain
Illustrated by Thomas Powell

The Edge of Carmel
Barbara Jean Chamberlain

The Sword of Smuggler's Point
Barbara Jean Chamberlain

A Slice Of Carmel
Barbara Chamberlain

Diana Chan
Letters Member since 2017

I was born in 1939 in Shanghai, China. On the eve of the communist takeover, our family moved to Hong Kong where we stayed for two-and-a-half years before moving to Sao Paulo, Brazil. I came to the United States for prep school and college, where I earned a BS in Early Childhood Education and a Master's Degree in Guidance and Counseling. I counseled high school dropouts in the South End of Boston, then became the Education Director of Head Start at the South End Neighborhood Action Program before retiring to become a full-time mother. In California I counseled homeless veterans going through PTSD at the Menlo Park VA. My husband and I are both retired and have traveled extensively. I have written and published two books, *Easy 'n Healthy Cooking Chinese, Fusion, & Western Cuisine* and *Animal Kingdom: Vertebrates, Animals with Backbones,* a picture book for children.

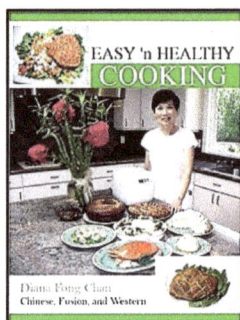

My interest in nature and wildlife inspired articles about swimming with whale sharks, and the "Amazing Octopus." I intend to use my writing to win support for wildlife, conservation, protection of endangered species, and environmental causes.

Writing is a good remedy for time spent sequestered at home during the pandemic. Since cooking and baking have always been my life-long hobbies, I have been creating new nutritious recipes using vegetables, fruit, seafoods, and meat packed with vitamins, minerals, and antioxidants. I would create a recipe, cook and take photos of the food in the backyard. Then I would enjoy the food with family or modify the recipe before sending it in for publication. *Los Altos Hills*, *Atherton Living*, *Mountain Homes*, and *Los Altos Town Crier* have published many of my articles and recipes these past two years.

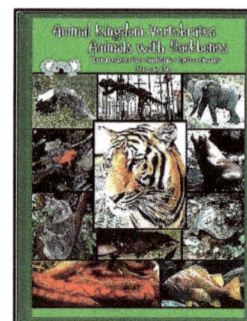

Pen Women are good role models for me because they are creative, productive and self-reliant. I have met artists, writers, and accomplished women who take on creative projects and stay active at home and in the community. They have also put me in touch with key people who have successfully published books and can help me continue to do so. Being a member of this group is an incentive to write, and they have helped me define my goals and the projects that I take on so that I use my time wisely.

Mary Miller Chiao
Letters Member since 2005

In 2005, I was honored as an Achiever in Letters at the Celebrity Luncheon held by the Santa Clara County Branch of the National League of American Pen Women. It was an impressive ceremony, and I enjoyed meeting all the members and seeing how talented they were. My good friend, Jeanne Carbone, suggested I join, and I have been a member ever since.

We have strong leaders, and I really like the other women in the group. Not only are they fun to be around, but they support my writing and have encouraged me to try new endeavors, such as photography. We meet once a month to discuss our fundraising and see an inspiring presentation by one of our members.

Once a year we have a large luncheon honoring women in the arts and we fundraise to provide scholarships. The luncheons are entertaining and informative, and I encourage everyone to attend.

I was born and brought up in New York and majored in American History at Syracuse (when I wasn't at the football games). In order to obtain my degree, I had to undertake a large research project. The hours in the library and in the field were time-consuming, but I loved the research, and that is an intricate part of my writing today. I've won awards for original research and my fiction has appeared in several magazines. I especially like the period of the 1950's.

Death on the Funeral Yacht, A 1950's San Francisco Mystery, is my first novel. It would never have been published if it were not for the support of our current Santa Clara Pen Women President, Luanna Leisure. My book is available at major bookstores and Amazon, both as a paperback and a Kindle eBook.

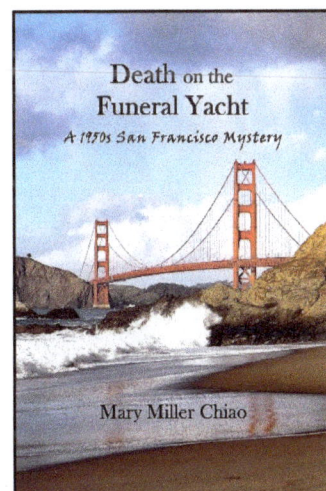

Cyra Cowa
Art Member since 2012

Being a Pen Woman since 2012, I have experienced the energy that comes from sharing artistic endeavors and ideas. I am enjoying getting to know very special people. We work hard to earn money to provide scholarships to give to future artists.

My paintings are an invitation to see through my mind's eye. My passion for oil painting has led to over 40+ years of professional work ranging from replicas to originals.

With the exception of my commission work, all my paintings are created out of my imagination—these worlds are externalized manifestations of my consciousness. The depth, atmosphere, and light in my paintings all reflect the inner feelings of serenity for which I long. The creation of these spaces has given me permission to breathe more deeply and feel more present.

After years of placing my identity in what I did for others, I had to find some way to express my "self." Through painting, I was able to discover a light within myself where I could find solace. Through the most tumultuous times in my life, I would paint as a way to meet with that light in me and learn to take command of it. It has been such a gift to know that others have received as much from my paintings as I have in creating them. To have the ability to welcome people into my world is truly a source of joy.

When people expressed an interest in owning my paintings, I entered Art and Wine festivals. Then I began showing in galleries. The latest are the Coastal Art League in Half Moon Bay and the John O'Lague Galleria in Hayward.

I especially enjoy doing commission requests by clients who have a personal choice in the subject matter and size. It has been my pleasure to offer my services as a teacher and coach to artists beginning their own creative path in oil.

I currently serve as Celebrity Luncheon Chair for the yearly fundraiser.

Patricia Dennis
Art Member since 2014
Letters Member since 2020

I am a California native, raised and currently residing in the Saratoga/Campbell area. An accomplished photographer, my style has been described by many as eclectic. My award-winning art has been on display in shows and galleries throughout the area.

My burning desire is that the final rendition of my images results in visual poetry that weaves hidden words, lines, dramatic color, and textures of the surrounding scene. Part of the fun and challenge is seeing what direction the photo will take. There is no doubt that the natural wonders surrounding us need no enhancement. However, when I look at a scene, I am always questioning whether it will remain a straight shot, or, will my heart dictate a different outcome. When the creative juices start flowing, the artist within often surfaces, creating an impressionistic version of the subject matter and adding subtle textures and color. I am often asked whether it is a photograph or a painting! Truly, the interaction between photographer, subject, and the viewer is a never-ending cycle that constantly inspires fresh outlooks and ideas within us all. Whether the scenes include wildlife, flowers, or landscapes; images and ideas from the emotional and physical world constantly fuel my passion for photography. With it, a desire to create images for future projects. It has been my pleasure to be on this journey and share it with others!

I've been a member of the Pen Women since 2017 in Art and Letters. I have served as Vice President, Publicity Manager, Web Site Manager, and on the Art Scholarship Committee. One of the things that attracted me to the club was being part of a group of creative women that give back to the community by providing scholarships. I also discovered a wonderful new world of friendships, shared ideas, and being with a group that understood the 'artistic' mind. Since joining, I have been encouraged to write. I am the author of three books: *Kerplunk*, *Dreamlight*, and *Chasing a Pink Cadillac*.

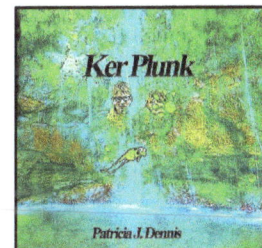

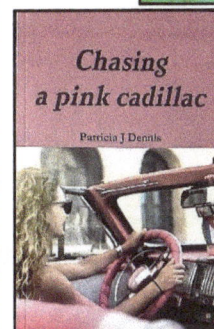

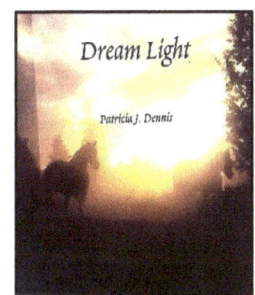

Patricia Watkins Dick
Art and Letters Member since 2009

Congratulations Pen Women of Santa Clara Valley, California. Yippee for this nonprofit and its dedicated members and leaders of the past one hundred years!

My Pen Women sisters help me set goals and bring them to fruition. I love my sisters and appreciate the outreach, concern, and love we have for each other. Honesty and inspiration churn the organization's spirit to reach out, shout, and cheerlead our members. We share the idea to connect and reconnect with one another. We instigate and support confidence and risk-taking in a safe environment. As Pen Women, our dozens of sisters enhance not only our womanhood, but also our creative souls.

I am a writer, vocalist, ballroom dancer, and artist. I specialize in watercolor and graphic art (crayons, conte, pencil, and ink) with a scrumptious attitude for exploring unconventional media and tools in new adventurous manners.

I am a graduate of the College of San Mateo, Peninsula Hospital Radiologic Technology School, DeAnza College, and San Jose State University. Education is a continuous privilege that I pursue. I am a retired Radiologic Technologist (an R.T.) and practiced for thirty years in my profession (one of my black and white art forms) while raising four children, primarily as a single mom.

I am a member of the Bay Area Creatives (formerly Arts of The Covenant), the Coastal Art League, and the National League of American Pen Women.

I donate my time, voice, art, and writing talents to support organizations, charities, senior citizen facilities, and PBS stations. These entities feed my passion for the creative process.

Kay Duffy
Art Member since 2013

A number of years ago, I was honored to be invited to become a Pen Woman by ShaRon Haugen. I very much enjoy the membership's diversity and their shared broad interests and talents. It has been stimulating to be a member.

I have been painting for over 50 years and have studied locally with Jane Hofstetter, Charlotte Britton, Jane Burnham, and Marie MacDonnell Roberts. I've painted in workshops with nationally known artists such as Brommer, Nechis, Szabo, Betts, Simandle, Webb, Cheng Khee Chee, and many others.

I'm an active member of the Allied Artists West, Santa Clara Valley Watercolor Society, Los Gatos Art Association, Saratoga Contemporary Artists, The National League of American Pen Women, and a signature member of the Society of Western Artists. I show regularly with these groups throughout the Bay Area. I also teach watercolor and collage in Los Gatos and give demonstrations throughout the area.

The freedom, spontaneity, and speed, the "wet and loose," of watercolor suits my temperament. My approach is "juicy," incorporating bright colors, broad strokes, and strong shapes to depict my feelings and impressions of the natural landscape, flowers and trees, buildings, foreign lands, and exotic places. Most enjoyable to me is the freedom of painting on location, *en plein air*. Inspiration for studio work comes from sketches and slides, taken while walking in the community, working in my garden, hiking in the wilderness, or traveling in foreign lands.

The City of Saratoga honored me by presenting one of my paintings to Saratoga's Sister City, Muko-shi, in Japan. In 2005 the County of Santa Clara purchased a local vineyard painting to present to their Sister County of Florence, Italy.

With my husband on sabbatical in 1993, I spent six months in Lyon, France, studying and painting. In the 1960s, we lived in The Netherlands for one year. We frequently return to Europe where I gather inspiration for my European theme paintings and sketches.

I am a native of Long Island, New York, and have a chemistry degree from Syracuse University. My husband is a retired physics professor from the University of Santa Clara. We have three children and three grandchildren. We've lived in Saratoga for over fifty years.

Rose C. "Pat" Fisher
Art Member since 2017

As a Pen Woman, I was initially surrounded by women who had continued to learn, teach, mentor, mother when necessary, and promote one another. They sought new women because their eyes were opened to the vastness of art, music in its many forms, and the written word. They sought me and now I am proud to be a Pen Woman. My passion and diversity of interests will continue to direct me towards like-minded artisans with new and exciting adventures. Thank you ladies. I am very grateful.

Growing up in Vallejo, California was everything it should have been: open space, cows, horses, dairy farms, parks to picnic, great neighbors who spoke to each other, and sports arenas.

My childhood was filled with music; because my dad was a terrific dancer, musician, cook, and self-taught wood sculptor. Whatever came on the radio the two of us would dance: Swing, Charleston, Waltz, Lindy-Hop, and I would easily follow my dad, laughing and making up steps as we went along.

Mom was a Tailor of men and women's' clothing as well as drapery making. My love of fashion comes honestly. When I began designing apparel, Mom encouraged me. When she began making the garments so I could see the finished product, I was hooked.

I loved playing the clarinet and went from 3rd Clarinet to 1st Clarinet in the Vallejo Symphony Orchestra. I was encouraged to try for the San Francisco Symphony, but I was turned down because I was only 16.

My creative expression never stopped. I was always setting goals. I liked sewing, music, jewelry making, gardening, cooking and sports. A family friend knew the Ebony Fashion Faire models and suggested I make jewelry for them. I did, and was happy they loved my designs.

Jewelry making was renewed after seeing the variety of beads and mentally putting colors and textures together. After a few years of beading, I started using the vintage fabric I had been collecting for years to design decorative pillows creating my own style. I was encouraged to have an Open Studio with a few friends and from there we were invited to participate in outside shows.

Geraldine "Gerri" Cynthia Forté
Letters Member since 2022

As a member of the California Writers South Bay Writer's Club, I am the new Managing Editor of the Writer's Talk Newsletter. I am honored to be a new member of the NLAPW. Edie Matthews encouraged me to join. The distinguished membership list is awesomely inspiring! As a retired educator, I now have time for recreation through friendships, encouragement, networking, and service work within Santa Clara County. We join forces to encourage younger females to expand their horizons, develop their creative talents, and productively share our minds and creative strengths as we forge ahead doing what we love to do.

As an Air Force brat, I was born at Hamilton Field Air Force Base in Marin County. I grew up in Vallejo and graduated from Vallejo Senior High School. I earned a BA in Behavioral Science and a MA in Counselor Education from San Jose State University. I earned a Doctorate in Organization and Leadership from the University of San Francisco.

My professional career as an educator spans Milpitas USD, San Jose USD, Merced Elementary SD, Ravenswood City Elementary SD, Tracy Joint Union HSD, Fremont USD, Santa Clara USD to the East Side Union HSD. I served these public school districts in the capacities of Teacher, Counselor, Site Administrator and/or Central Office Administrator. Upon retirement from the public school system, I taught Masters level courses in the Education Department at the National Hispanic University, and supervised student teachers at Santa Clara University. Now retired from the field of education, I spend my time writing, growing roses, baking cakes, and loving my two Chihuahuas.

My four published books:

Appropriating Old Cultures Into New Futures - From The Kingdom of Tonga to the State of California (1995), Of Prayers and Beatings (2019), The Sinceria Pound Cake Extraordinaire - A Recipe for Life (2021) https://www.youtube.com/watch?v=1rpLOhPJ9L0&t=13s, A Brand New Song to Sing (2021) https://www.youtube.com/watch?v=YvrQ8mmehlM, A Pandemonium of Parrots - in progress.

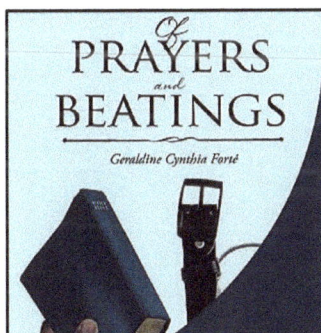

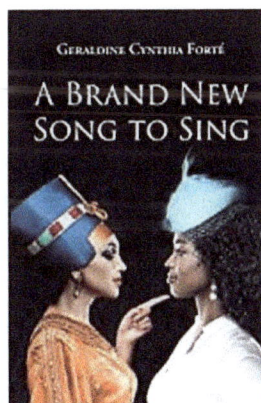

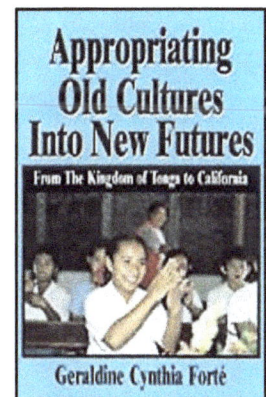

Karen Franzenburg
Letters Member since 2017

I have been a Pen Woman since May of 2017. I joined under the Letters category. I am enjoying getting to know the women in our Santa Clara Branch and networking with them. They all are so friendly and willing to help one another.

Since becoming a member, I have been able to publish my first book: *Just Say Yes!* It is a chronology about the stroke I experienced in 2016. One of our members assisted me in its publication. That experience and listening to the other writers in our branch, has me working on my first novel.

I am also trying to find time to enter my photography and art into some of the shows our artist members exhibit in.

Being involved with the Pen Women is a unique experience. It makes me want to create. I would encourage other women to join. They definitely would not regret it.

Lorraine Gabbert
Letters Member since 2020
Art Allied Professional Member since 2021

Being a Pen Woman means being part of a joyful sisterhood full of talented individuals who are an ongoing inspiration. Jeanne Carbone and Kimberlie Brady introduced me to Pen Women. I attended the Pen Women Luncheon in honor of Brady's award, and later Carbone invited me to a meeting.

I am a freelance reporter and photographer covering city news and local politics for San José Spotlight and the Almaden Times. I bring years of writing experience to the job, including articles for 90210, b.a.b.y, Bay Area Parent, LG Magazine, San Jose Magazine, the Mercury News and South Bay Accent.

I previously worked in film and video production in Los Angeles and for the American Broadcasting Company in New York. I studied journalism at Pennsylvania State University, and film at the New School in New York.

During the pandemic, I turned to art, writing, and poetry to fill my days and lighten my mood. I found it meditative, and relished the creative process.

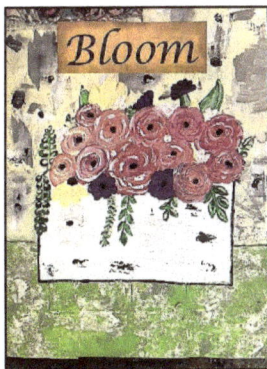

Standing By

Shadows reach across curving roads
Towering trees, age old sentries
Silently stand guard
Surveying softly rolling hills
Cloaked in verdant down

Mountain Call

Majestic peaks reach for the sky
Its craggy face
Armored in angular stone
Challenges climbers to
Feats of bravery

Dianne Glass MacNair
Letters Member since 2001

My mother told me I could do anything I wanted in life, but I needed a college degree and a wealthy husband. I didn't take her seriously! In high school I enjoyed drawing, photography, writing poetry, and singing in the chorus, church, and with a local band. I also attempted to play the guitar and piano. I was in the Drama Club and loved acting. High school was boring, so I decided to graduate in three years. I took extra and summer classes. Success…

My first serious attempt at supporting myself after high school was working part-time and attending the John Robert Powers Modeling School. After graduation, it didn't take long for me to realize I wouldn't be on either the New York or Paris runways due to my short stature and large bust. Reality hit, and I quickly realized a college degree was the alternative to being broke. I followed my passion for creativity, combining it with a practicality for business, and received two Fine Arts Degrees and an MBA. Also, I earned several two-year certificates which including Technical Writing, Project Management, and Gem and Diamond Certifications from the Gemological Institute of America, plus many other shorter programs that supported my career.

Between all those pursuits, I served in the Army and was stationed in Bamberg, Germany, and the Presidio in San Francisco. There were so many opportunities in Silicon Valley. I had an interesting and successful career in management working on top secret programs, managing multimillion dollar projects, supervising people from secretaries to PhDs, all while learning the latest technology. I filled my creative dreams with a part-time jewelry business, painting, writing, and music.

I have been in the NLAPW for twenty plus years. Pen Women are the most creative, ambitious, delightful, individualistic, competitive, cantankerous, and wonderful group I've ever been associated with. We speak when needed and are never shy, silent, or passive when it affects our passions.

I met Judith Fabris in 1998 when she moved into the cul-de-sac where I lived. We became fast friends, as did our husbands. We spent many wonderful years together traveling, writing, partying and living a fun life until she moved to Southern California. I was a first-year technical writer when we met. She encouraged me to join the NLAPW and do more creative writing. We formed several writing groups over the years and always had a great time. I've learned so much from all the Pen Women in every state. I especially enjoyed the Biennial Conventions.

I am currently married to my soul mate and love of forty-three years, and we live in the beautiful foothills of Reno, Nevada. Life is Wonderful!

Alice Ann Glenn
Letters Member since 1982

Being a Pen Woman has brought me many years of socializing as well as some very serious friendships with an amazing group of professional writers, composers, and artists. When I was first hired as a contract writer with my denominational publisher, I had tons of support, and publicity, about my writing, all due to Pen Women.

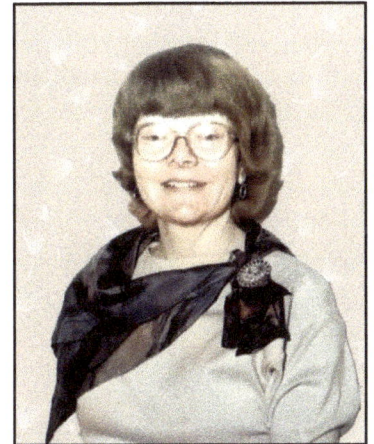

One of the things I greatly appreciate with Pen Women is the encouragement at regional events by this group to "cross over" and create something in a category different from the one that I originally joined with.

Besides being a contract writer for twenty years of writing children's curriculum and a wide variety of articles related to Christian Education, I was the Editor for my District denominational newspaper and memoirs for the annual conference; and editor for a variety of colleagues' books.

All of my life, including a graduate school paper, I have done collage. Since living in Monterey, I have done some assemblage, focused on the threat to the ocean from all that is found on our streets that go into storm drains. I also make cards for all occasions by recycling used greeting cards and other ephemera.

The New Forest

Microwave receivers
huddled together
atop a hill.
Like the old seeders
left on clearcut mountains,
these modern seeders breed--
eavesdropping.

Claudia Gray
Art Member since 2018

I am a multi-media artist and have received recognition and awards for my art, photography, glass work, and jewelry. My work has been featured on Fox News, and recently, I was a featured guest on a TV show where I discussed my art and my life as an artist.

I have received many awards for my artwork and photography, including "Monet's Giverny" from the Triton Art Museum Show and "Archway to the Past" from the juried all-media Coastal Arts League Gallery Show. I'm a prolific artist and my work is simultaneously exhibited in numerous galleries, museums, juried art shows, and is sold at various retail establishments. My largest order to date was to create 450 glass surfboards and platters for the St. Regis Hotel in Southern California.

My photography and articles have been published over fifty times in newspapers and national magazines. I live and work in the Bay Area and am inspired by nature and Eastern philosophy. I care deeply about the environment, and I live and create with eco-friendliness in mind. In 2017, I volunteered six weeks for the National Park Service in Yosemite National Park. I currently serve on the Board of Directors for the Coastal Arts League Gallery & Museum and on the Board of Directors for The Los Gatos Youth Parks Council. I have created under the names "Claudia Gray" and "Patricia M. Gray."

I was first introduced to the National League of American Pen Women by Judy Bingman. I saw her at shows where we both exhibited. She always encouraged me to join the group. Finally, because she was so persistent, I decided to become a Pen Woman, and I am super glad I did. In February 2019, I received an award from the National League of American Pen Women in recognition of my Achievement in Art.

I feel like I am surrounded by very talented ladies who are producing quality work in publishing, art, photography, and music. It is an inspirational group and a great network of creative people.

Carol Greene
Letters and Music Member since 2000

I have many interests: performing ventriloquism with puppets, composing music, playing piano, taking pictures of scenery and people, writing, traveling, attending symphonies, reading books, watching movies, dancing, and laughing with friends.

I became a Pen Woman after Susan Zerweck, who was president at the time, asked me to participate in the Celebrity Luncheon. At my first meeting as a member, I became secretary. I was assistant chairman of the Celebrity Luncheon when Susan was the chairman.

Music has always been a vital part of my life. I grew up in a Chicago suburb and Denver. At sixteen my mom helped me open my piano studio. I also learned ventriloquism and performed at four birthday parties every weekend. I paid all of my college expenses at the University of Denver. During my Junior year, I got married, and dropped out of school. My business grew. After my husband graduated, we moved to the San Francisco Bay Area. Two years later, I graduated from San Jose State University. During my thirty-three-year teaching career at the Moreland School District, I used my puppets to teach. I taught Grades 4, 5, and 6, then became the district's first Creative Arts Specialist. During this time we had two children of our own. I took early retirement from teaching in 1997.

Friends call me Ambassador of Good Will because I have taken puppets to six continents and all the way across the U.S. when my husband rode his bicycle across the U.S. During my two trips to Japan, I performed in Japanese. My puppets and I taught English in China. Firefighting equipment was purchased with the proceeds of my performances in Belize.

I enjoy singing, dancing, and walking around with my puppets. I have appeared on radio, television, and stage. I was a columnist for *LaughMakers Magazine* for ten years. I performed for all nine Las Vegas International Ventriloquists Festivals. I composed and directed a musical called *Noah's Ark* with the children's choir at Skyland church.

Currently I enjoy taking pictures of people and scenery. I have directed, sung, and played percussion with Elbon Singers at senior facilities. A day is special when people smile or laugh with my puppets and me.

email: carol@carolgreene.com, Website: www.carolgreene.com

Travel blog with my photos: www.carolgreene.com/travel

Phyllis Gunderson
Art Member since 2015

As a decade-long Member of the National League of American Pen Women, I credit this organization for the growth of my artistic abilities and confidence in sharing and selling my art. I joined when I was making the decision to engage in turning my avocation into a vocation. This group was instrumental in that decision and I will be forever grateful.

I have always been on the move. Growing up, we moved often, as my father was an Air Force officer. This gave me a wonderful exposure to the many beautiful cultures and places. I think my appreciation of the beauty of the landscape had that early origin. Everywhere you look, there is beauty both seen and felt.

My art training has been largely self-directed. I pursued my art studies outside my academic training in Public Administration and Systems Engineering. I had a rich and varied career ranging from Law Enforcement to Executive Management in High Tech. I was able to return to my first love of painting about ten years ago and have been exhibiting nationally for nine years. My work is collected in the U.S., Canada and in the U.K.

Two years ago, I was fortunate to be challenged to try painting en plein air. Wow, what a wonderful door to open and explore. Outdoor painting has completely changed the way I see and understand the world. It forced me to start over and appreciate anew this beautiful world. What better place than in the singular beauty that is New Mexico. Yes, I'm hooked. My husband and I reside outside Pecos, New Mexico.

I belong and am active in the following artist organizations
- American Impressionist Society
- Arizona Plein Air Painters
- National Association of Independent Artists
- National League of American Pen Women
- New Mexico Art League
- Pecos Studio Tour, Chair
- Plein Air Painters of Colorado
- Plein Air Painters of New Mexico, President
- Oil Painters of America
- Outdoor Painters Society
- Rio Grande Art Association
-
- Humming Wolf Studio
- https//:pagunderson.com
- Email: pagunderson@att.net

ShaRon Haugen
Art Member since 1992

I was invited by Dori Phifer to a meeting of the NLAPW in 1992. I was very impressed with the mission of the League to promote development of the creative work of professional women in Art, Letters, and Music. The Santa Clara Branch raises money for high school/college women in the arts who use these scholarships to further their achievements. We also honor individual women who have achieved professionalism in their field at a Celebrity Luncheon each year.

The professional women in this group are impressive. We work at getting the word out about our branch and the mission we have.

"Paint it all" is what I really do, from flowers to old wood. I enjoy painting, every stroke from start to finish. Choosing challenging work is a habit of mine. I work primarily in oils, but also do scratchboard of animals. This technique is black and white. With a pin-like tool, I scratch on a white clay board surface with black ink on top, removing the ink to show white lines from underneath. This makes it look like hair on animals.

Born in Utah and then moving to Washington State, I spent my youth on a farm. After moving and traveling with my family for several years, California became our home in 1972. It was here that I began my serious oil painting, studying under many art instructors.

Living in the country inspired me to paint the lonely old barns and buildings of the rural area. Indians and Old West paintings stem from my fascination with history. Springtime brings out my flower painting mood.

I became a professional artist in 1975, and for many years, I traveled extensively with my art. My paintings have been displayed in art shows and galleries throughout the western region of the United States.

Sheralee Iglehart
Letters Member since 2006

Education and reading have been very important to me throughout my life. I learned from my mother who taught in a one room schoolhouse in Nebraska, and continued to teach into her 80's.

I have Life-Teaching Credentials in two states: New York and California. I have taught elementary school full time in the Bay Area, California, Ithaca, New York, and Omaha, Nebraska.

I received a scholarship from Stanford University for a Masters in Education which I pursued for a year before getting married and moving to New York. I later completed my Master of Arts in Reading Education and California Credentialed Reading Specialist, Notre Dame de Namur University, Summa Cum Laude in 2008.

I am a member of the National Scholastic Honor Society, Delta Epsilon Sigma, having received a B.S. in Education, Elementary Education and Teaching, University of Nebraska-Lincoln.

My 5 books include *Cough In Your Shirt, Bert*, *A Very, Very Special Birthday*, *Three Cheers for Kangarooslow*, *Mommy, Baby and Me*, and my latest book, *10 Proposals and 10 Diamond Rings*.

I am married to a Stanford Professor, Donald Iglehart, and have two sons, both of whom are graduates of Stanford University.

Since joining in 2006, it has been an honor to be a member of the NLAPW, the oldest women's arts organization in the United States. Through the NLAPW I have been able to network and develop lifelong friendships with talented and incredible women which has been a continued source of inspiration. Website: Sheralee.com, Email: sheraleeig@gmail.com

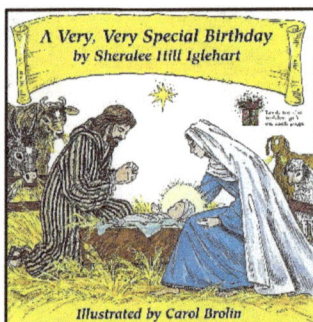

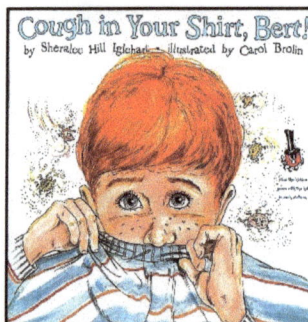

Marjorie Johnson
Letters Member since 2015

I taught high school mathematics in Santa Clara for thirty years. During that time I served as secretary and treasurer of the Fibonacci Association, which publishes the academic journal, *The Fibonacci Quarterly*. I also wrote and published 89-plus peer-reviewed articles on the Fibonacci Sequence. I have also been on the FQ Editorial Board since 1963.

When I retired from teaching, I pursued my lifelong dreams of learning to fly, traveling the world, and writing novels. I started by traveling to Mexico and taking creative writing classes from Edie Matthews to learn how to write a good story.

While visiting Mayan ruins with archeologists, I learned that the Maya had a complete system of writing, similar to that of ancient Egyptians; but the Spaniards burned Mayan libraries during the Spanish Inquisition. The skill of reading Mayan glyphs was lost for several centuries. Archaeologists have been able to read most of it since the 1990's. I had found that "really good story," the basis for *Jaguar Princess: The Last Maya Shaman* and the sequel, *Lost Jade of the Maya*

. How did I become a Pen Woman? Edie Matthews and Susan Zerweck invited me. I enjoy the group because every time we meet, the very air crackles with creativity and good will.

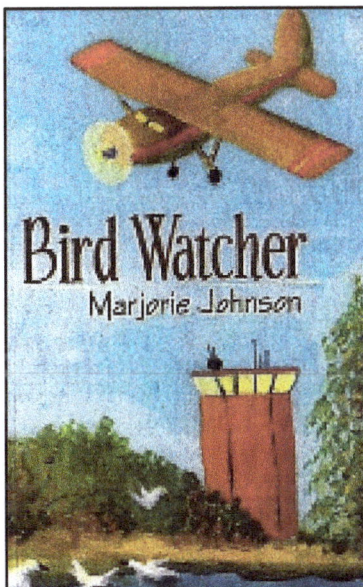

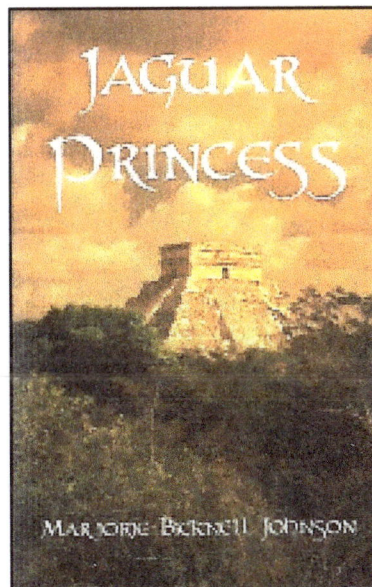

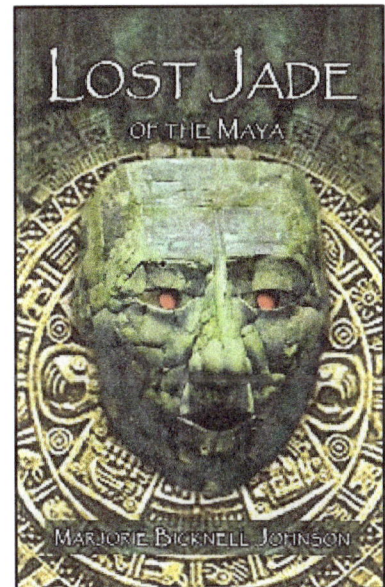

Lorna Kohler
Music Member since 2018

I was invited to join the Pen Women after the 2016 release of Wishbone Drum: my second collection of original songs, for which I performed vocals, guitar, oboe and English horn. One of my daughters played cello on one of the songs. My other daughter provided the cover photo and spent hours listening with me for the sequence of the songs. At that time I was still playing oboe and English horn in three orchestras, as well as teaching voice, piano, and a variety of string and wind instruments to students.

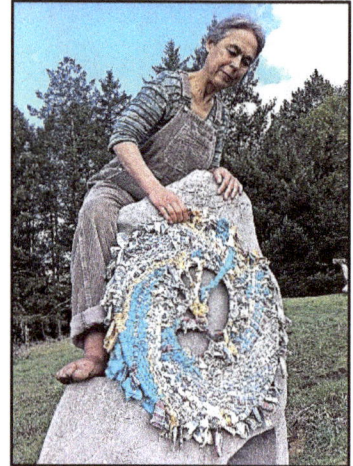

When my daughters were two and four years old, I made a shield out of shirts I had worn when I was pregnant with them, tearing them into strips and tying them onto a hoop made from a branch from a rose bush in my garden, on which I left the thorns. Thirty five years later, it hangs on my wall, with the shape of a fetus formed by the negative space in the center and a turquoise braid like an umbilical cord attached to the golden cuff of a shirt, with the button in the button hole at the center.

I wrote a song, inspired by a dream that came to me during the making of the shield, and choreographed a dance to it. I included it in Winter Calls, my first collection of original songs, released in 1987. This song flew all around the world:

> Spiraling into the center, the center of the shield
> Spiraling into the center, the center of the shield
> I am the weaver, I am the woven one, I am the dreamer, I am the dream.
> I am the weaver, I am the woven one, I am the dreamer, I am the dream.

I experience the Pen Women as an amazingly diverse group of women, with a shared love of creative expression, in whatever form it takes in our lives. I am inspired by individual Pen Women who find or invent creative forms to help them transform challenges in their lives, or to give expression to whatever brings joy and beauty and meaning into their lives. This is also an extremely caring and compassionate community. During the years that I have been a member, we pass through the river of life together, with some of us so fully alive, no longer here with us in their bodies, and new women coming in.

I have been amazed to learn that a conversation I happened to have with a member has continued to be a source of inspiration and encouragement for her. I have been touched by the outpouring of handmade cards and loving thoughts during a year when I have experienced the deaths of many loved ones.

Here are lyrics to another song I composed:
> Spirit breathe through me, that I may remember who I am and why I am here
> The sap of the one tree sings inside me from roots that go back before the beginning
> All my relations, the stars and the stones, echo the singing I hear in my bones
> Spirit breathe through me, that I may remember who I am and why I am here.

All of my life, I have been exploring the mystery of who we are and why we are here, through music and words and dance and ceremony and the magic of creative process. I collaborate with an unseen source to give form and expression to the wisdom and beauty seeking to come through me from eternity into this world of time and space.

Carolyn Larsen
Art Member since 2015

I have a BA in Art Education and have been teaching art for over 25 years. My classes are in watercolor, oil, and pastel, and all mediums. I went to Lincoln High School, Seattle, Washington. I studied Art education at the University of Nevada in Reno.

Traveling to Florence and Tuscany, Italy with "Welcome to the Renaissance workshop tours" led by Dr. Sam Hilt and Pam Mercer were wonderful adventures and learning experiences. Visit my website at www.clarsenart.com.

Luanna K. Lynch Leisure
Letters Member since 2012
Art Member since 2020

Photography, writing poetry, short stories and pencil drawing is what I have been doing since I was a preteen. My eldest sister gave me her hand-me-down Brownie camera and I took it everywhere with me taking pictures. I didn't know I was writing my memoirs until I met Pen Woman, Louise Webb who invited me to her memoirs class.

I first came in contact with Pen Women over 30 years ago in Visalia, California, where I worked at College of the Sequoias as the head of the Scholarship Department. These lovely ladies gave monetary awards to young women talented in the arts.

Fast forward to 2012 and living in Campbell, California I came in contact with a SCC Branch Pen Women, Ursula Meir. I got so excited when she said she was a Pen Woman. I had good memories of the ladies in Visalia. Ursula was kind enough to read my first manuscript, giving me a positive critique. It wasn't long after that until Ursula invited me to a meeting. Shortly after that I was actively involved in the Santa Clara County Branch.

I love being a Pen Woman. At the very first meeting I attended, I knew that I was with ladies I could relate to: Talented ladies with imaginations, ideas, full of talent in all areas of the arts. Audry Lynch, Mary Lou Taylor and Ursula encouraged me to get my first book published. Without their positive and helpful attitudes and seeing what the other Pen Women were accomplishing, I would have never become a published author.

In June of 2017 I was invited by National President, Virginia Campbell, to participate in the NLAPWs 120th Anniversary celebration in Washington, D.C., where it was an honor to make a presentation on one of my children's books.

If there was a moto that describes me it is: "More Ideas Than Time." I am always thinking and I can visualize a story outline in the most unexpected objects, experiences and places.

I have published three children's books: *Mystery at Lone Oak Ranch, Quack! Quack! I Want My Feathers Back!* and *Best Buds.* I have also published *Best of Our Memoirs,* a book of memoirs written by Louise Webb's memoirs class. I've written, *Ledra's Book*, a book honoring my mother, and this book on the Santa Clara County Branch Centennial Anniversary. All of my books are available on LuLu.com and Amazon.com. My website is LuannaLeisureBooks.com

In 2020 I earned my art credential in photography. Finally, my love of taking photos paid off.

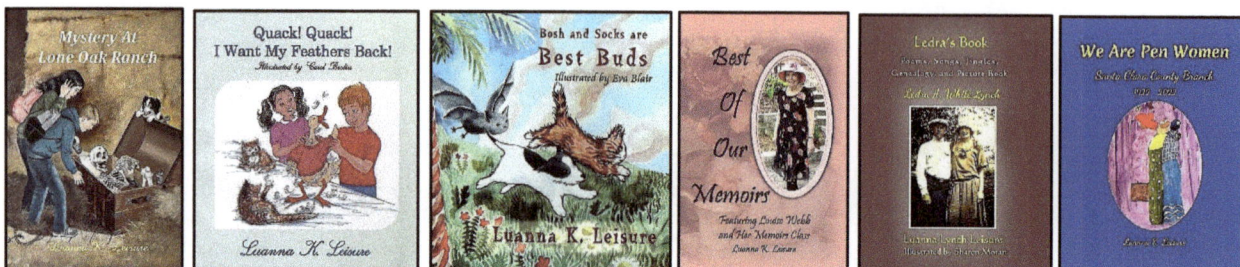

Genevieve Liu
Art Member since 2021

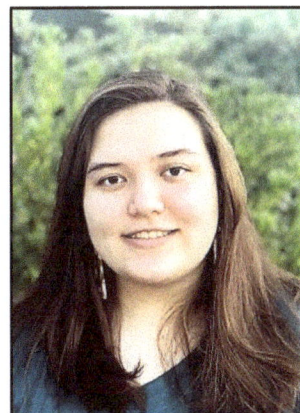

Though I've only been part of the Santa Clara branch of the National League of America Pen Women for a few months now, I can't express how inclusive and fun these ladies are. From the beginning, Luanna has been sweet, funny, and overall a wonderful person to be around! I am so happy she encouraged me to join. When I finally got to meet most of the Pen Women, I had a wonderful time. Age doesn't matter. We all shared lots of laughs, stories, important ceremonies, and food. I'm so glad to be part of such an amazing group that supports each other and has fun.

My main goal in life is to make an impact on this world, ideally with my art. I want to explore every type of art that can help me express myself clearly, more and more, to the point where I'm satisfied. Art to me has always been about communication and point of view, no matter what level, media, and skill. I want to be remembered. I want my art to make people think. I don't want to end up in the category of being purchased for social class recognition. I just want to be me and be seen as such.

I have received some awards in the arts. During my senior year, I submitted an AP art portfolio, half of it showing a story about growing up and the other half showing the breadth of my work. I got the perfect score of five out of five. I also submitted one of my pieces from that portfolio to an art contest where I won, and it was put into a small exhibit at the San Jose International Airport. My art has been shown in the CUHSD Art Shows over the years. The high school art teachers choose which student's works will be displayed for the school district to see.

I just started attending college at the University of Hawaii in the Fall 2021, majoring in art. I'm learning so much and loving it.

Gail Lockhart
Letters Member since 2020

I was continually looking for an association of women who wanted to give back to the community. I joined group after group, but none of them met my expectations until someone invited me to a meeting of the Pen Women. I finally found a community home of like-minded women. We encourage each other and inspire each other to grow, but mostly, we give back to the community by supporting the arts and providing scholarships to talented young women. Art is such an important way of expressing ourselves and giving beauty to the world. Thank you, Pen Women!

I started working in stained glass in 2015. I fell in love with it, and to my utter surprise, I became very good. Yes, it took practice and many cut or burned fingers, but I prevailed, so much so that I now have a work studio outside of my home where I design and create. I teach classes in stained glass as well. Anyone who wants to learn is welcome.

My philosophy on stained glass is simple. I want the world to know that if you design and create your own pieces, it is no longer a craft but an art. This is what I do. To help people who want to own my work but have small budgets, I price my art affordably.

I wrote my first book after I retired from my financial advising business. During the sixteen years that I owned my own company, I realized that parents do not talk to their children about finances. So my first book, *Timmy and the Money Tree*, is about Timmy and his family going on a tour of the Bureau of Engraving and Printing (which, by the way, cannot happen in real life).

My second book is titled *Timmy and the Ice Cream Man*. In this book, Timmy learns to make change. All of my books have been illustrated by both my husband and me. There will be more coming about children being financially knowledgeable at a later date.

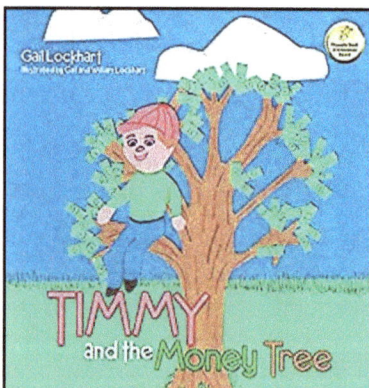

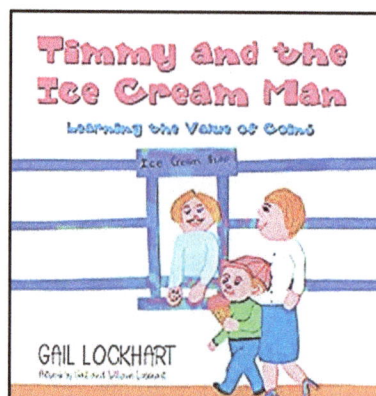

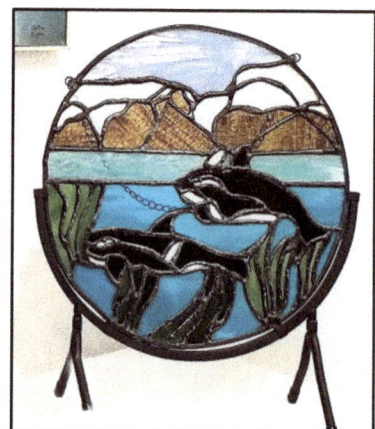

Audry Lynch
Letters Member since 1995

In 1970 my family moved from Boston, Massachusetts, to Saratoga, California. We changed cultures and climates almost overnight it seemed. After many years as a working woman, I was suddenly a stay-at-home mother. It didn't take long for me to realize I needed something to help with all these adjustments. I saw a small article in the local newspaper about a club called "Pen Women." Since I loved to write, I thought this is the group for me. It promised friendship, support, and workshops on writing. It delivered on all counts.

I made lasting friendships, was "mentored" by veteran members, and received constant encouragement. From being a former freelance feature writer, I graduated into writing books, seven in all. I wrote a Steinbeck Collection, taught classes, and organized tours of Steinbeck Country. Twice I won the nonfiction prize at the annual Pen Women National Conference. I was delighted when the women from my branch joined me at the award ceremonies. My involvement in Pen Women helped to make all of this possible.

We celebrate the good times together and try to help each other through the bad times. Unlike other clubs, we talk shop and share ideas about improving our talents. It's a club with a diversity of voices for all seasons and all kinds of creativity.

I am so glad I found you! Thank you, Pen Women!

Here is a list of my books:

1. *With Steinbeck in the Sea of Cortez*
2. *The Rebel Figure in American Literature and Film: The Interconnected Lives of John Steinbeck and James Dean*
3. *The Development of Roy Simmonds as a Steinbeck Scholar as Evidenced through his Letters: The Life and Achievement of an Independent Academic*
4. *A Priest in His Parish*
5. *Steinbeck Remembered*
6. *Garth Jeffers Recalls his Father, Robinson Jeffers: Recollections of a Poet's Son*
7. *Ruben's Tales from the Amazon Jungle*

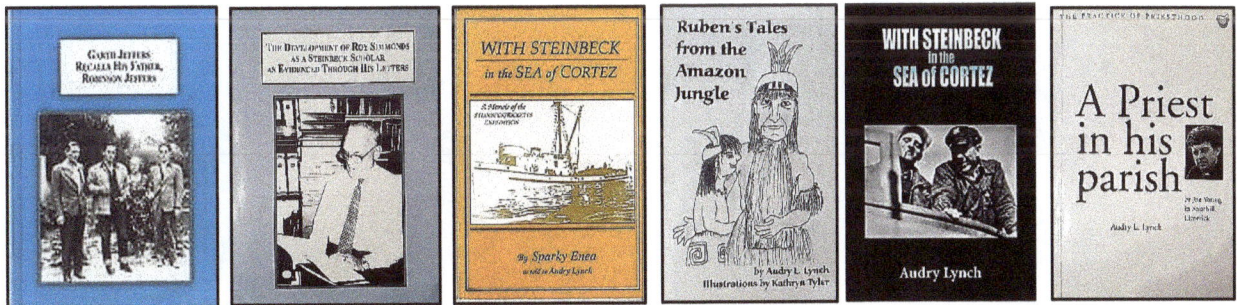

Edie Matthews
Letters Member since 2001

Even after twenty years, the talented ladies in Pen Women continue to amaze and inspire me. Our social events are always festive—whether it's our Celebrity Luncheon honoring local women or the New Members Tea—which I love hosting. Many of our occasions encourage costumes and themes, providing opportunities for our gifted ladies to express their creativity.

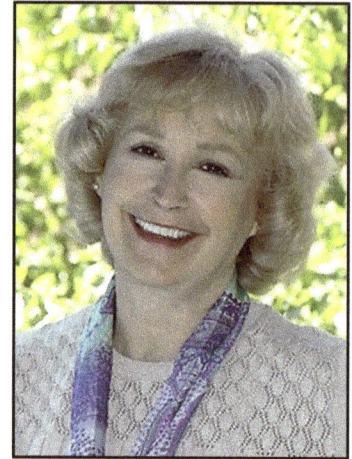

My experience includes working in print, radio, and TV newsrooms, as a tech writer in Silicon Valley, and a standup comedian. In comedy clubs, I rubbed shoulders with Dana Carvey, Ellen DeGeneres, Jay Leno, Rosie O'Donnell, Robin Williams, etc.

While living in Los Angeles, I finagled a story in the *LA Times* (twelve comedians living in an old Hollywood apartment building). With my comedy neighbors, we wrote several pilot scripts, met with producers, a production company, and the Vice President of TV Development at Columbia Studios. But showbiz is fickle, and executives keen on the idea were replaced, promoted, or entered rehab.

Undeterred, I created a comedy show, *Mothers & Other Goddesses*, and toured the US and Canada with a partner on the "No Stinkin' Dishes Tour."

Penning a humor book, *You've Been Around Small Children Too Long When...*, inspired my interest in writing. After earning an MFA in Creative Writing at San Jose State University, I began teaching English and Literature at De Anza College. I'm currently the President of the South Bay Branch of California Writers Club and have co-directed four East of Eden Writing Conferences set in Steinbeck Country (Salinas, CA). Presently, I'm remodeling a historical house and writing a novel inspired by my odyssey in the World of Comedy.

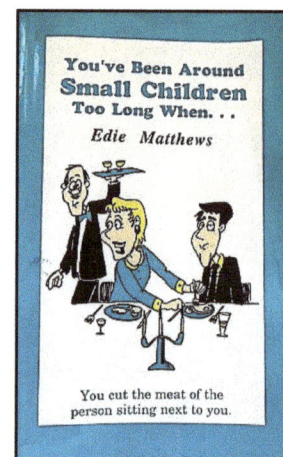

Jana McBurney-Lin
Letters Member since 2017

I was born in Chicago, Illinois. But, after graduating from Bates College in Maine, with a degree in Rhetoric and a minor in Japanese, I went off to live in Japan. I only intended to stay a year (to brush up on my language skills with the hopes of going into international business). But, then I fell in love with the culture. And, then I wanted everyone else to learn about it. I ended up staying six years, where I wrote for magazines, journals, and newspapers in seven countries. I also met my husband, a native of southern China, and we moved to Singapore for eight years. During one of our trips home to his village I ran up against a compelling story, this time one that deserved more space than an article would offer. Thus I started writing fiction.

My Half of the Sky (KOMENAR, 2006) is the story of a contemporary young woman who is trying to be modern--to hold up her half of the sky, as Chairman Mao dictated women should--but the traditions of her village keep pulling her back. While the narrative takes place in China and Singapore, the theme is universal. How do we reconcile traditions with the modern momentum of our society?

Soon after publication, while signing books at a writers' conference, a Korean engineer approached me saying, "Your book reminds me of old Korea. Will you help me tell my story?" Dr. Hi-Dong Chai grew up in Seoul prior to WWII, as the son of one of the first Christian ministers in a country that was ruled by Japan…and thus, Shintoism. As a result, his family was always under persecution. *Blossoms and Bayonets* (Redwood Publishing, 2013) is based on his story.

Ever since returning to the U.S (San Jose, CA) in 1999, I've been involved with writing organizations. I've been a member of the California Writers Club since that time (serving as President of the Peninsula branch for five years.) In 2008, after the publication of My Half of the Sky, a friend suggested I join Pen Women saying, "*You need to be connected to a National Organization.*" I've always been grateful. I am constantly amazed by the talent that abounds, the instant and warm reception from all the members, and the support offered to future Pen Women.

I continue to write fiction (and am still massaging a draft of a sequel to My Half of the Sky.) However, the bulk of my time is spent writing technical non-fiction for Western Digital. I live with my husband in the Santa Cruz Mountains, and we have four grown children. My hobbies include hiking, traveling, and reading to children.

Ursula Meier
Letters Member since 1995

I started writing after being inspired by my writing class teacher, Erna Holyer, who was a member of the National League of American Pen Women. Erna has since passed away, but her enthusiasm and writing style continues to inspire many women. Weekly critique groups have formed that carry on writing in Erna Holyer's tradition.

It is wonderful to be together with talented and intelligent women, going in the same direction, ladies I can relate to, with whom I feel at home.

I have written articles for the American and German newspapers and magazines. I've been nominated for and received many awards. The United States Congress awarded me the Certificate of Special Congressional Recognition, and I was named Outstanding Immigrant to the United States. For my thirty years' work as Director of Education at German-American Schools, I received Germany's highest citizen honor, the Order of Merit. I was nominated for the Hawaiian Book Award, received the Eudora Welty Memorial Award, was invited to speak on television, and have had many interviews. I was also a freelance researcher for the Hoover Institution of Stanford University.

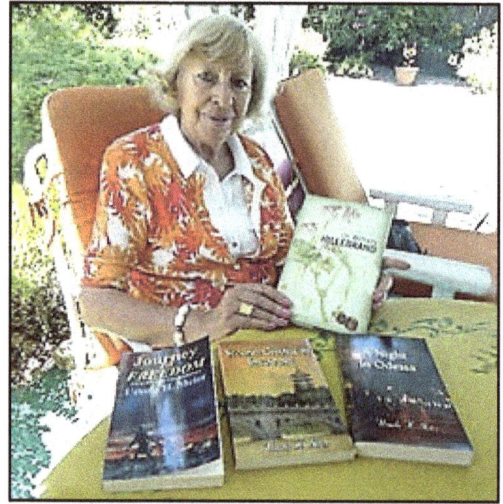

I have published five books, with a sixth in the final stages of editing.

- Hawaii's Pioneer Botanist, *Dr. William Hillebrand, His Life & Letters*
- *Journey to Freedom*
- *A Night in Odessa*
- *Second Chance in Singapore*
- My fifth book is a sequel to *Second Chance in Singapore*. The title is *The House on the Hillside.*
- My sixth book is *Call to Rome*

My print books and e-books may be purchased on Amazon.com and Barnesandnoble.com

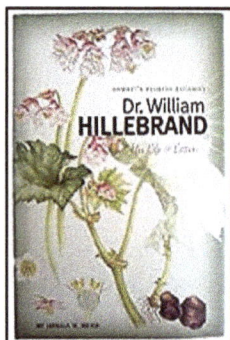

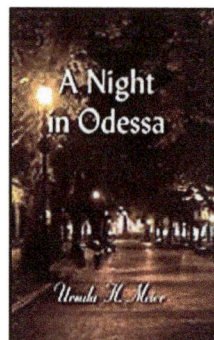

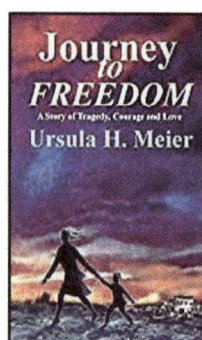

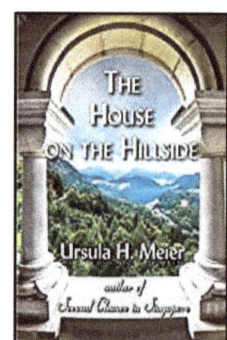

Maralyn Miller
Art Member since 2003

I am so honored to be a member of this wonderful organization of talented women who have achieved amazing accomplishments through their published books, art, and music.

These women have been an inspiration to me, just knowing them.

Originally from Fresno, California, I received my BFA from the California College of the Arts in Oakland, California. Following Art School, I moved to the South Bay where I owned and operated three art supply and picture framing stores for thirty years.

I have constantly pursued my art career and have been showing and selling my paintings from 1959 until the present. The subjects I used have been various, but mostly they are realistic depictions of California in oils and pastels. My work is in private collections of over six hundred people and institutions.

Tola Minkoff
Art Member since 1999

As a member of the NLAPW, I continue to meet many creative women. Reading writers' publications, seeing artists' creations, and hearing musicians' performances have been very stimulating. I enjoy being a Pen Woman.

I lived in Los Angeles with my parents before moving to Palo Alto. Since I was in my twenties I have been interested in the arts. Because I especially liked sculpture, I took a class in sculpting at the Chouinard Art Institute. I've also expressed myself through watercolor, chalk and oil pastels.

When I met Judy Fabris at a meeting in San Jose, I shared my small sculpture of a seated woman. Judy encouraged me to join her Palo Alto Pen Women branch which was then called *Las Artes*.

While taking a class at Palo Alto's Pacific Art League (PAL), when they used live models, I sculpted a reclining nude. I made two casts. I donated one to a PAL auction which brought in $240.

In a NLAPW show, I received first prize, a yellow ribbon, and a certificate in the Sculpture category for my four-year-old boy.

Currently, I pursue oil pastels and have completed a few outdoor scenes and a portrait of a British nanny and her ward.

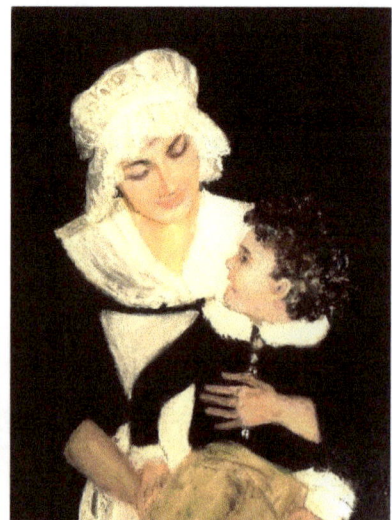

Carolina L. Mueller
Art Member since 2012

Ever since childhood, I have been inspired by the creativity and art of all cultures. Over the years, I have tried silk painting, watercolors, acrylics, quilting, crocheting, window-glass art, mosaics, decoupage, Ukrainian egg painting, and so much more. I have received many awards for my art. Creativity is my life. I'm always on a quest.

I am fascinated with the stained glass and cut glass of the medieval centuries. You can see the effect of the Middle Ages on my silk work. I use silk as my canvas and try to get the stained-glass effect by employing different kinds of resist. Why silk? Silk is a wonderful medium and can be used for many purposes. It is challenging to paint on a lustrous and smooth surface. Its texture and glow are unsurpassed. I love to use bright and vibrant colors which help to enhance the depth of the picture. To achieve brilliant colors, I use the finest European silk dyes. All painted silk is hand washable. I make beautiful scarves and shawls.

My friend, photographer Judy Bingman, invited me to a NLAPW Santa Clara branch meeting where I showed my silk art. She nominated me to be a Pen Women Achiever in 2012, and I was honored at the Celebrity Luncheon of the Santa Clara branch. I displayed my silk art on a table, and it was very exciting. I met all the members and realized they were a sophisticated and talented group. It was an honor for me to become a member of such an established league! Receiving the Vinnie Ream Merit Award was probably my highlight in recognition, and I loved participating in the Biennial Conference.

Over the years, I've felt the love, the support, and the opportunities this group gives me. So much to learn and exchange! It surpassed what I knew and was used to. The experiences made me grow.

Most of all, I love the fact that we support growing artists with scholarships. All the effort, love, and determination by our members to make our Celebrity Luncheons enjoyable and successful fundraisers gave me a purpose.

I was born and raised in the United States but spent 28 years in Germany before moving to California in 1999. The natural beauty of Europe inspires me with its beauty, as does California, and the Hawaiian Islands. In 2019, I returned to Germany, but I love the Pen Women and maintain my membership in the Santa Clara Branch. I miss being with everyone.

Janie Oberhauser
Letters Member since 2021

The Pen Women are a diverse collection of writers, musicians, and artists from all walks of life. Members of each branch both support and advise each other and foster an appreciation of the arts in the greater community. I haven't been a Pen Woman for long, but my favorite parts so far have been the group's empowerment of female artists and the warmth and enthusiasm with which I have been welcomed.

Storytelling is my passion, whether through fiction or scientific journalism. I wrote my first children's book, *The Mystery of the Missing Socks*, during the pandemic and hope to publish more in the future. Luanna Leisure invited me to be a Pen Woman after helping me publish my book. It is available for purchase at Lulu.com or on Amazon. I am currently writing my first novel.

I graduated from the University of North Carolina at Chapel Hill in 2021 with degrees in Quantitative Biology and English.

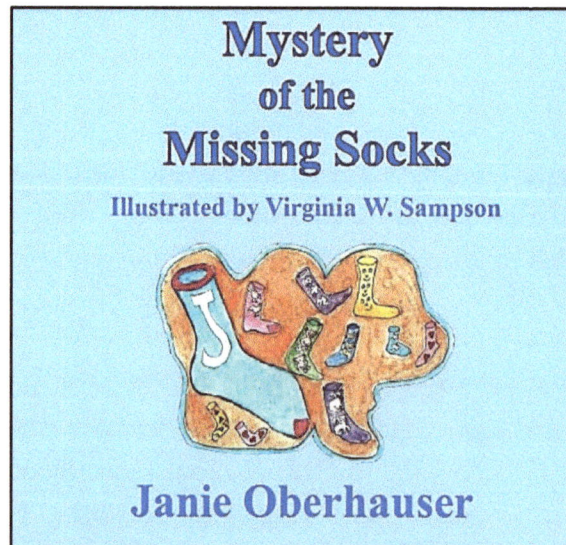

Mystery
of the
Missing Socks

Illustrated by Virginia W. Sampson

Janie Oberhauser

Kathy Olson
Letters and Music Member since 2011

I am the founder of The Children's Play House, a non-profit corporation located in San Jose, California. Children in grades K-8 who are enrolled in the program receive acting, singing and dance instruction which culminates in performances for a paying audience. A CD of the music and costumes are provided for each child. The main goal is to build self-esteem in all children regardless of talent. As Executive Director, I write all our material which is age-appropriate for children and includes a character-building moral in the story.

I started writing musicals for children forty-seven years ago. To date I have written over forty musicals and included in every work at least ten are original songs. All songs are written in an easy to sing range and often are catchy and fun. It is fascinating to see the children bring the work to life!

In addition to my work at The Children's Play House, I started the Theater Arts Program at Castillero Middle School in the Almaden Valley in San Jose, California, a Performing Arts Magnet School in the San Jose Unified School District. I taught Theater Arts for 25 years at that site, retiring in 2002. I graduated with a BS from the University of Minnesota and a Masters degree from San Jose State University.

I live with my husband, Terry, Captain USN, Retired, and our two Lhasa Apso dogs. Our three children are married, and we have seven grandchildren and two great-grandbabies.

Jane Parks-McKay
Letters Member since 2011

I love being a Pen Woman! I was honored to be named an Achiever at the Santa Clara Branch's Celebrity Luncheon. Words cannot accurately express my feelings when Ariel Smart introduced me and talked about my writing and accomplishments. I immediately joined the Pen Women, sponsored by my friend Audry Lynch, and I am glad to be in the company of these amazing women. We Rock! Our group has talent, diversity, and dedication to the cause of promoting women through our networking and our scholarships.

I wrote a popular book called *The Make-Over, a Teen's Guide to Looking and Feeling Beautiful* (published by William Morrow and Company, 1985). It was an outgrowth of my teaching at the private school I owned for twenty-one years. I created the marketing plan for my book and implemented it. I still run into people who tell me my book meant a lot to them.

I had always wanted to be a teacher and a writer. When I was around thirteen, in Alabama, I wrote a beauty book and sent it to *Highlights* magazine. When we lived in Georgia, I started a charm school for the little girls who lived next door. They were AWOL a lot so I set up a classroom to teach from my Dad's work museum about the space program. I had my kitty cat and stuffed animals as students. I also started writing a newspaper for the family.

After I retired from teaching and promoting my book, I returned to college to change careers to law. I loved it. It took me twenty-two years (while working) to get my college degree. I majored in a pre-law course of study and intended to transfer to Santa Clara Law School, but we bought a house in Capitola. There were so many repairs needed that we had no money for law school. The owner of a lovely tearoom in Capitola, and other businesses, asked me to help promote them. For seven years, I ran a public relations business. I had a lot of clients, but I specialized in hospitality.

For a number of years, I was a freelance writer for area newspapers and was nominated for a Pulitzer Prize for a piece I wrote about a part of Highway 280 at Saratoga Avenue which had been dedicated to an Officer. It ended up being an article on post-traumatic stress. I included a sidebar with ways that people could get help.

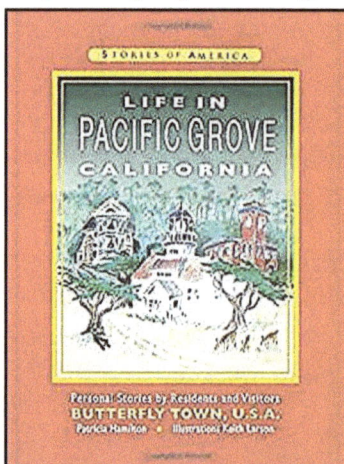

I was a longtime member of the California Writer's Club where I met and became good friends with Audry Lynch. Together, with a few others, we spent three and a half years traveling around as a community service group. We performed as the Traveling Steinbeckians to help raise awareness about literacy as well as honor native son John Steinbeck. We had the full blessing of the Steinbeck family.

In 2007 my husband became ill, and, for nine years, I became his full-time caregiver. We were interviewed by the media about traumatic brain injury, caregiving, etc. Eventually we did presentations together. We both created a new normal. My husband is a prolific artist. I still write and have won many awards.

116

Elvira Rascov
Art Member since 2021

I am a watercolor and ceramic artist from Colombia, South America. Currently, I am a member of the Aegis Gallery in Saratoga, California, where I sell my ceramic creations. I love to teach, and, at the beginning of 2020, I started to give watercolor classes at Los Gatos-Saratoga Community Education and Recreation. Because of the pandemic, I am teaching different watercolor projects online through Zoom. It has been different not to have students in person, but I have managed to accommodate my classes with this new teaching method. In the new year, I will return to in-person teaching.

These past three years have been an art journey. I have participated in different juried exhibitions through the Los Gatos Art Association and also at Coastal Arts League Gallery in Half Moon Bay. It has been a rewarding experience for me to see my watercolor and oil paintings being accepted on juried exhibitions. Also, this past year, I illustrated a book, *Bubbe, the Wind and Me*, by Norma Slavit, another member of the Santa Clara County Branch of the NLAPW. It was my first time illustrating a book, and I enjoyed the experience.

I became a member of The National League of American Pen Women in February, 2021. My friend, Marcia Sivek, told me about the organization. I was amazed the first time I attended one of their meetings. I believe what attracted me to become a Pen Woman was the encouragement and support of the group. It wasn't easy to fulfill all the requirements to become a member. I didn't have the number of juried shows required on the application. Still, with the guidance of Dorothy Atkins, ShaRon Haugen, Patricia Dennis, Luanna Leisure, Cyra Cowan, and others, I applied to different juried shows. During this process, I acquired a better level of confidence with my art and had fun at the same time.

It is an honor to be a member of the National League of American Pen Woman. All the Pen Women are professional and involved in their artistic fields. Together we showcase our art and share the same interests. I have found an excellent support network of professional women in the arts.

Mary Ann Savage
Letters Member since 2016

I was born near Charleston, West Virginia. I attended West Virginia University and the University of Pittsburg, Pennsylvania earning my Master's Degree in Psychology.

Through the years, I have been busy writing. I wrote a play, *Women's Territory*, which was performed at Cabrillo College. I had stories published in the journal, *Rambunctious.*

To my delight I have received numerous 1st place awards and an honorable mention for my published poetry. These are just a few:

- *Perseids*
- *Widow's Walk*
- *Requiem*
- *Capturing the Unicorn and*
- *Hospitality*

I co-authored a book, *Cotton and Spirit.* Currently, I am putting together a collection of short stories, poems, and I am experimenting with chapter books. I am also in the process of revising a book based on experiences working in a residential treatment center.

I did live in Watsonville, California and attended Pen Women meetings, but I now live in Virginia to be close to family. I am still a member of the Santa Clara County Branch.

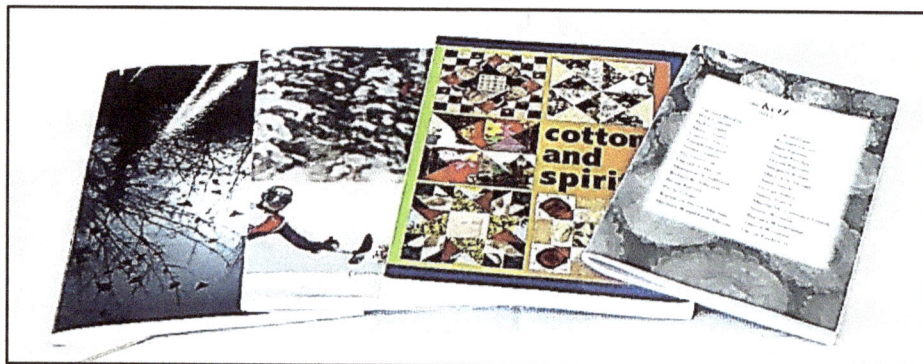

Geraldine "Jerri" Scaife
Art Member since 2000

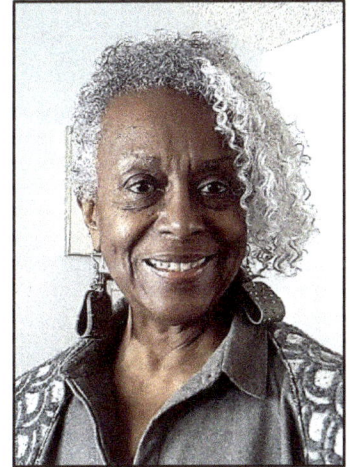

I am a textile artist and fashion designer. I first tapped into my gift at the age of 12, inspired and mentored by my aunt who designed costumes for exotic dancers.

I didn't choose this work, it chose me. It was my passion, it was so much fun! I just took it and ran with it.

I am lucky that I am not afraid to step out and take chances. I always feel free to experiment and do something different. Some of my best creations have come from mistakes. That is just part of the creative process. I have actually had the experience of someone loving something so much and wanting it so badly, that they bought it right off my back. I love to make people happy.

I'm intrigued and fascinated by unusual fabric. Helping others to embellish their wardrobe and enhance what they already have is what I do best. And I'm not talking mass production. For me, it's all about one-of-a-kind creations.

Someone once saw me at a show and said, "Jerri, are you still at it?" I looked at her and said, "This is something I will always do. When I stop doing it, please check my pulse. I don't think you'll find one."

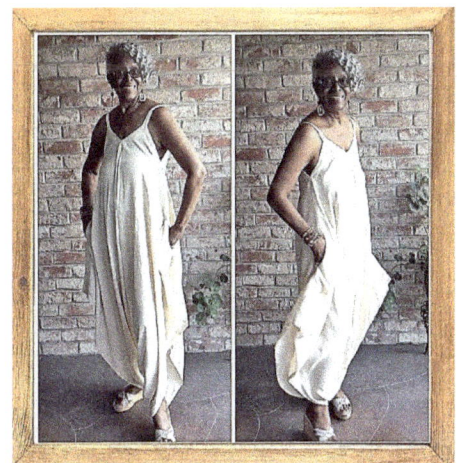

Marcia Sivek
Art Member since 2017

I was introduced to Pen Women while sitting on a large pile of bags of birdseed at Los Gatos Birdwatchers - part of an art show supporting the arts and birds. As ShaRon Haugen and Patricia Dennis sat on either side of me, they talked about an amazing organization that supported their advancement in the arts. I soon joined Pen Women.

I've been an Artist in the Santa Clara County Branch for four years. During most of this time, I've served as the secretary. It's been an honor to be on the board with amazingly talented women.

I've always loved drawing horses, peoples' faces, facial contours and muscular structures. While I was in college and working (geological engineer, environmental engineer, nutritionist and patient coordinator), my art went by the wayside. In 2015, when I found myself without a job, I began volunteering with the March for Elephants which helps ban the cruel use of elephants in circuses.

When I realized I could express my love for animals through art, I enrolled in a watercolor class and began teaching myself how to draw elephants, birds, and cats. During the pandemic, after I painted a snow leopard cub in oil, I gave prints to the Snow Leopard Conservancy which raises money to help protect snow leopards and their environments.

In 2017, at a wildlife conference, I met Dr. Laurie Marker, the founder of the Cheetah Conservation Fund. She asked me to work on education and cheetah conservation in Namibia. After returning to the U.S., I started a podcast called Be Provided Conservation Radio. By interviewing conservationists, scientists, artists, authors, and volunteers in rehab/rescue centers, I built a 3000+ audience within four years.

Now, my podcast is on hold as I seek to open a science and nature store which will focus on bird watching. The store will be a safe, fun and educational place where people learn how to feed birds they have in their backyards, and how to help them thrive. I'll also sell art relating to birds. I hope to open it by summer 2022.

Norma Slavit
Letters Member since 2012

Pen Women's diversity of talents is wonderful. We're motivated, like-minded, supportive, kindred spirits. I enjoy being with women who share a love for writing, music and art.

I was a Master Teacher in elementary schools in New Rochelle, N.Y. and San Francisco. I taught music at Hillbrook, a private school in Los Gatos. For thirteen years, I was a Newspaper Editor for the Jewish Community Center in Palo Alto. My articles have appeared in educational journals and newspapers. I published a play, and an early story appeared in the Encyclopedia Britannica reading series.

I am a member of the Society of Children's Book Writers and Illustrators. My first book, *Peaches, Frog and the Man in the Moon* is a picture book for children ages four to eight. *The Elephant Who Had Allergies* is for children of all ages. *September Thanksgiving* is a chapter book for the middle grades. *Pork Buns and High-Fives* is a chapter book for middle school children. It is based on the memoirs of an Asian boy who grew up in Silicon Valley. All my books contain an educational component for teachers and parents.

The Rabbi at Temple Emanu-El in San Jose wrote the foreword in my latest book, *Bubbe, the Wind, and Me.* Rabbi Dana Magat writes, "This sweet, magical story brings to light the precious nature of the grandparent/grandchild relationship, focusing on what is most important—sharing our time and our love with our Bubbe (Grandma)." Good role models, acts of kindness, looking for the good in people, and making wise decisions are threads I weave into the tapestry of my books.

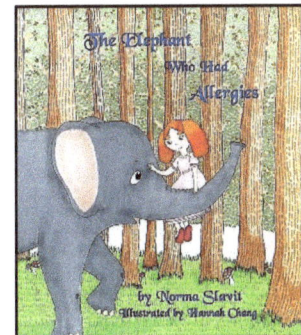

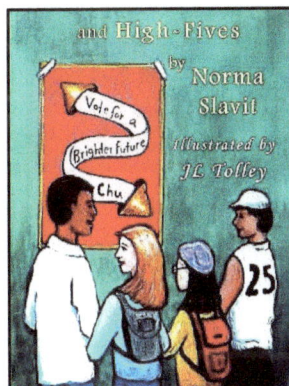

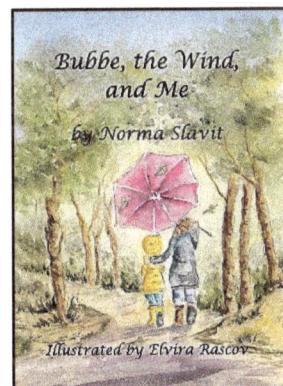

Ariel Smart
Letters Member since 2007

I love being a Pen Woman because I meet interesting, stimulating women of the arts who come from all backgrounds and give me insights into this transitory world. Mary Lou Taylor sponsored me.

I have published many poems. In 2020, I won the Lamont Poetry Prize. My publications include *The Green Lantern and Other Stories*, published by Daniel & Daniel, available on Amazon.

WE NEVER STOP COMING OF AGE. My characters take risks, make choices, change, and grow.

As I demonstrated in my earlier collection, *The Green Lantern and Other Stories*, I am a keen observer of the human heart. Many of the stories in The Green Lantern concerned a young girl's coming of age. My most recent collection, *Stolen Moments and Other Stories,* is an even richer exploration of the human heart, demonstrating that loss of innocence is not limited to childhood, and that coming of age is a lifelong process.

I was born in El Centro, California, in 1936 to Frank Leroy Davis and Esther Tilbor Davis. Five years later, my brother David was born. My parents owned the Green Lantern Motel on Highway 66. My grandfather, Frank John Davis, lived with us. It was he who introduced my father to my red, curly-haired mother who sold Band-Aids to businesses. My parents eloped to Mexicali, six miles across the border from El Centro. My father was a thirty-four-year-old bachelor. My mother was twenty-nine years old.

In 1946, my parents moved to Pomona, California, where we rented a lovely house for three years. My father became a carpenter. My mother, born in New York of Polish Jewish parents, continued working as a door-to-door saleswoman. She rode a blue Schwinn bicycle she called "Angel".

I was introduced to Pen Women by Mary Lou Taylor, and it is a pleasure being a member of Pen Women.

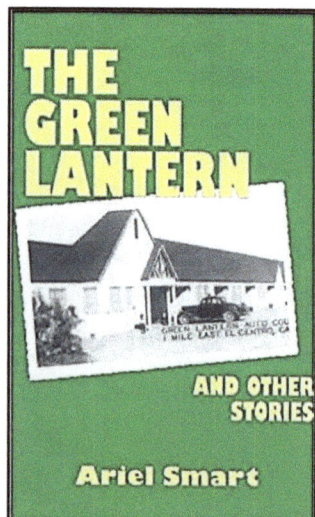

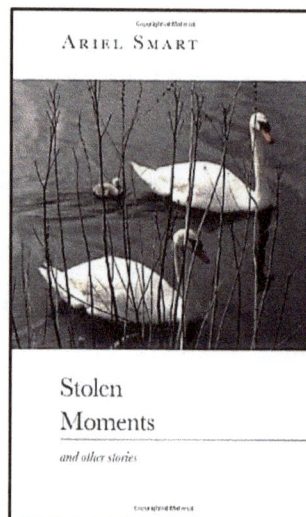

Bonnie Jo Smith
Letters Member since 2016

The journey began for me when I met a NLAPW member at my neighborhood park one day and she excitedly talked about the Santa Clara County branch.

Her excitement and information about the Pen Women really piqued my interest. Several years later, even though I have moved away from the area, I am still a member of the Santa Clara County branch. Belonging to a women's organization that focuses on all the arts is important to me.

I also appreciate how my art has been recognized at the national level of NLAPW. My talent is textile arts, sometimes called fiber art. My textiles are about "what I see and know," interpreted as meaning I focus on the environment and family. My textiles have traveled the globe, received a lot of recognition, and have been placed in many private collections.

Even though my work is centered on art, I have also authored two books, *Through the Eyes of a Child* and *Swimming Upstream a Memoir*. Both books are about my own personal journeys. A third book I authored, *She Votes*, is about the celebration of the 19th Amendment. In that book, I feature sixty-four artists' works on the subject.

With so many talented and wonderful women as members of Santa Clara branch of the NLAPW, it is a pleasure to belong to this organization. www.bonniejofiberarts.com

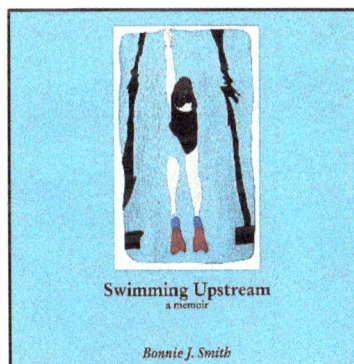

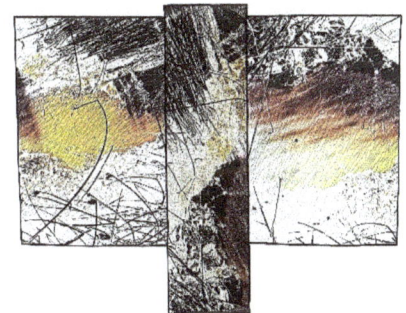

Patricia A. Suggs
Art Member since 1987

Ever since I have been part of the Pen Women, I have made some very special friends. The meetings and social get-togethers with the ladies were delightful. Unfortunately, it has been difficult to attend meetings these last few years because of my husband's illness. However, the Pen Women are what keeps me going!

A third generation Californian, I am a noted pastel artist and resident of San Jose. Drawing and painting since childhood, I feel that the Crayola Company has started many an artist on their life journey. My formal art training was at the Leighton Fine Art Academy in San Francisco, and I have focused on the art of pastels over the past forty years. Traveling the world, I have acquired visualization knowledge of art and art history at the great art centers, such as Paris, Florence, Amsterdam, Dresden, St. Petersburg, Copenhagen, Istanbul, Madrid, Sidney, and Shanghai, to name a few.

A full-time artist, I am known for my expressive floral, landscape and seascape paintings, and my ability to capture light. I am a **Master Pastelist** member of the Pastel Society of America, NYC, and was inducted into the International Association of Pastel Societies, Master Circle, in 2005. Prestigious venues around the United States have displayed my work, e. g. Butler Institute of American Art, Ohio, The National Art Club, NYC, Binney & Smith Gallery Banana Factory, Bethlehem, PA, Triton Museum Fine Art, CA. I have had paintings published in *Best of Pastel* and *Floral Inspiration,* Rockport Publishers. I have been listed in *Who's Who in American Art* since 1993. For nineteen years, I have been treasurer for IAPS. Private collections represent my work throughout the USA and France. You can view my artwork at Gallery 24, www.lggallery24.com, located in downtown Los Gatos, 24 N. Santa Cruz Ave., Los Gatos, CA 95030.

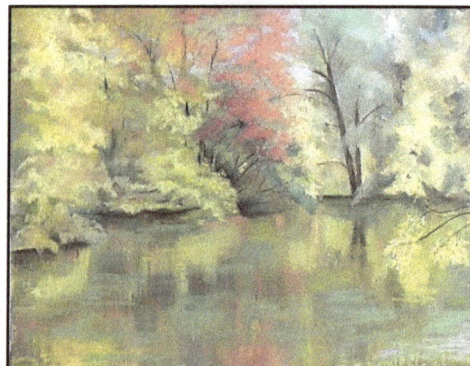

Mary Lou Taylor
Letters Member since 2001

I would like to begin at the beginning, when my dear friend Felicia Pollock said I should join the Pen Women. The first luncheon I attended I won three wrapped baskets, and I've been with the Pen Women for the past twenty years. I am in a wheelchair now, but in those years I've met members who have become close friends, and I have gained an appreciating for art and music which has become part of my life – alongside my poetry. Over the years I've watched the branch grow.

Writing poetry began when I was eight years old, inspired by my father who always read to me *David Copperfield.* When asked, I have said, "It's just in me to write."

For more than seventeen years, I have been a dedicated member of the Santa Clara County Branch of the National League of American Pen Women in Letters. I have mentored and encouraged many new members as well as poets and my students during my career as a high school teacher.

For thirty-seven years, I have served Poetry Center San Jose, in numerous capacities, including two terms as president. I have participated in open mic poetry readings at the Willow Glen Library, contributed to programs, events and many fundraising activities.

In 2002, with the encouragement of PCSJ members and the assistance of an attorney friend, a contract was written and accepted by the CEO of History Park, San Jose, to make Markham House their headquarters. **A** historic San José landmark, the Markham House is a Victorian home where the famous poet Edwin Markham lived in the late 1800s. The house is used by PCSJ to host adults and children's poetry workshops, poetry festivals and open house events.

I was editor of the Abby Niebauer Memorial competition and I currently serve as a trustee emerita of the Center for Literary Arts at San Jose State University.

Throughout my years of writing, I have received honors, awards and invitations to recite. My love of poetry becomes contagious to those who feel my emotions as I recite from the pages of my books. I have the ability to mold my past experiences into well-crafted poetry.

A native of Chicago, I grew up in Los Angeles, a setting that inspired my first poetry collection, *The Fringes of Hollywood*, published in 2002 by Jacaranda Press, San Jose, California, which recalls my time living in Tinseltown. I have several poems in *The Call: An Anthology of Women Writers*, Dragonfly Press, Columbia, California, published in 2009. During my residency at Montalvo Arts Center in Saratoga, I received my inspiration for writing, *Bringing Home the Moon,* published in 2015 by Aldrich Press. *In the Beginning*, my newest book, featuring ekphrastic poetry set to fourteen paintings of renowned American painter, David Park.

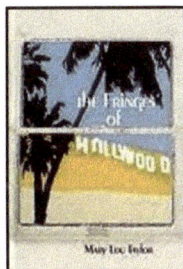

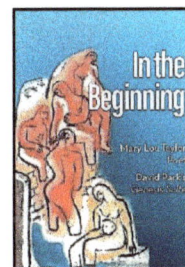

Lori Howell Thompson
Letters Member since 2020
Art Allied Professional Member since 2020

I am proud to be a member of the NLAPW organization. NLAPW thumbprints what is important to me: to reach women of all ages and open the door to them for opportunities to explore their talent as writers, artists, photographers, and more. Most importantly, NLAPW isn't only a national organization, it's family. The women throughout the organization are my mentors, teachers, sisters, and leaders.

I am the author of three books: a thriller, *Reflections*, and two children's books, *An Adventure with Joshua and Hoppy* Frog and *An Adventure with Joshua and Rocky the Otter.* I illustrated *An Adventure with Joshua and Rocky the Otter.* My children's books are in three elementary schools in Salinas, and I've started a reading program in many California schools. A two-page article featured me in the 2017 *Women of Distinction Magazine*.

My screenplay for *Reflections* has won thirty-seven awards inclusive of film competition and contest awards as Best Thriller.

I am also an award-winning artist and enjoy painting landscapes, seascapes, nature, and creating murder scenes within a painting. I love to create paintings to "Tell the Tale." My paintings have been exhibited in both Assembly Member Anna Caballero and Congressman Jimmy Panetta's art exhibits.

I want the characters I create in my stories to come alive; and in my paintings to mesmerize the observer. My genres are landscapes, seascapes, nature, waves, mixed media, and illustrations. I love the mystery of finding stories in everything and everywhere when in the midst of a writing project, I enjoy researching plots. My mind dazzles with ideas. Writing inspires painting, and painting inspires writing. Woven together, they create a love story.

I owned the Reflections Elegante Fine Art Gallery in Willow Glen, San Jose, until the Covid shutdown.

My greatest joys, besides painting and writing, are being a wife, mother, and grandmother. Lake Tahoe, New Zealand, and Carmel are favorite places.

Personal Quote: "I Live to Create and Create to Live!" https://inawritersmind.com/painting

126

Judith "Jude" Tolley
Art Member since 2018

I first met several members of the Pen Women when I was in a show at the Coastal Arts League in Half Moon Bay, California. There were several members included in the same show, and I was struck by how supportive they were to each other. When I heard more about the organization, I knew I wanted to be a member. The group includes visual artists, musicians, and writers, all creative and innovative artists. One of the best things about this group is that the members have diverse interests and all are professionals. I was inspired by the poetry and the music and, of course, the life story of each and every member in the group. All are professionals who have an impact on a wider audience through published writings, music, and other creative outlets.

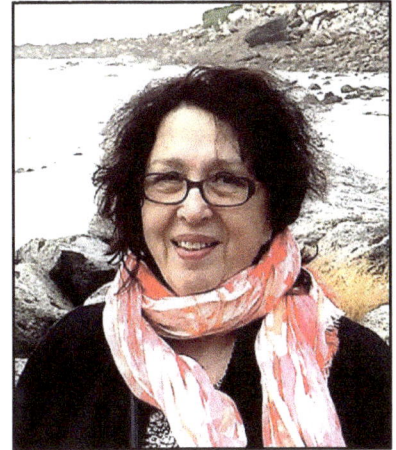

These gatherings always inspire my own creativity. I feel I have found a community of like-minded folks who are intent on supporting each other in pursuing their own creativity as well as sharing the creative energy with each other.

I grew up in Virginia and spent a great deal of time in the Washington, D. C. museums. My father and my grandfather were master calligraphers so I grew up with the sound of their pens on the paper. I watched them carefully burnishing gold on their illuminated documents, and these experiences had a profound impact on my awe of creating something on a blank piece of paper or parchment. I found their art inspiring.

I attended Virginia Commonwealth University in Richmond, Virginia, graduating with a degree in painting and printmaking. I then furthered my studies by attending classes at the National Academy of Design in New York City. I apprenticed with painters, Dani Dawson and Nelson Shanks. Additionally, I studied sculpture with Bruno Lucchesi. Always fascinated with how things move, energy in motion, I worked for many years in the animation industry, including at Walt Disney Feature Animation. Wanting to share the art of storytelling through animation, I pursued and received grants from the D.C. Commission on the Arts in Washington, D.C. to introduce art programs into several D.C. schools. Students from seven schools produced animated films which were collectively shown on WETA-TV (PBS) in two specials entitled "A Capital Kids' Celebration of Animation" and "A Capital Kids' Celebration of Animation II."

Currently I am a member of the Santa Clara County Branch of The National League of American Pen Women, The Coastal Arts League, and the Campbell Artists' Guild.

Kathryn A. "Katy" Tyler
Letters Member since 2012

What I love about the pen women is that each is unique in her talents. It is what shapes them and makes them so special. My definition of creativity has broadened and become enriched since being a member of the National League of American Pen Women. I'm proud to be in their company.

I'm from San Mateo, California. I went to college at Willamette University (in Salem, Oregon), Harlaxton University (in Grantham, Lincolnshire, England) and San Jose State University, majoring in 4+ subjects. For 35 years, I was a schoolteacher, mostly in the middle schools, teaching Writing, Art, Math, Physical Education, and during the last two years of my career I had the pleasure of co-teaching with my husband, Randall, who was the band teacher. I especially enjoyed learning the band instruments!

I've always loved writing, art and music. I was in the Salem and Santa Clara Symphonies as a violinist; and I drew, painted, and wrote as often as I could. My biggest written work is *Drums in the Hills,* a book that I wrote about my grandfather and Pancho Villa, (a famous Mexican revolutionary). It is the post pandemic 'queue' for a movie production.

Other interests I have include hiking (I've climbed Mt. Whitney three times), biking, animals, and Scrabble (continuing my love of words).

My 40-year-old daughter, Kim, is a former model and now runs a nonprofit animal organization called "Army for Pets". I am secretary of this organization and enjoy volunteering at animal shelters she sets up in disaster areas where animals are vulnerable and need help.

128

Bonnie Vaughan
Letters Member since 2001

I discovered the Pen Women when my friend, Eloise Kintner, nominated me as an Achiever for a technical manual, the *Ada User's Guide*. I was nearly nine months pregnant with my third child. As I received my award on stage at the Saratoga Country Club, Eloise stood ready to drive me to the hospital, if necessary.

My software development team at Tandem, where I worked for many years, told me the *Ada User's Guide* was my first science fiction novel because I wrote it before the software was developed. We used text from a similar document, with permission, to prepare the book in time for our software release. I put all of their names on the book as authors, and they loved it.

My first real science fiction book, *Spaceborn*, was published years later by Black Opal Books, after my friend Bonnie Hearn Hill recommended the book to the editor.

After I joined the Santa Clara County Pen Women branch. I went to meetings because Eloise asked me to, and she encouraged me to keep writing fiction. I also published a short story, "An Unexpected Blessing," in *Things that Go Bump for the Holidays*, an anthology by Black Opal Books.

I just finished a young adult science fiction novel, *Acacia*, which I wrote because my oldest son, Chris, asked me why my name wasn't on my technical books. He helped me edit and market *Spaceborn* and created a web site for it at bonniegvaughan.com. So I put his name on this book in the dedication. Now it's standard practice for companies to put authors' names on their technical books.

I'm halfway through writing a sequel to *Spaceborn*, titled *Mars Quarantine*. Because of my books, I attended National Mars Society Conventions where I met famous science fiction writers. I gave them copies of *Spaceborn* to thank them for their stories, and they insisted that I sign the copies for them. The next day I saw the cover of *Spaceborn* on a slide in a presentation about women science fiction writers.

I'm retiring from my tech writing job at Oracle this month so I can write many more science fiction stories for you.

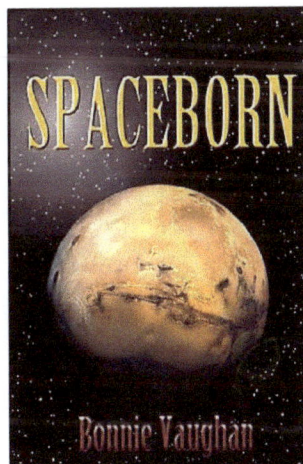

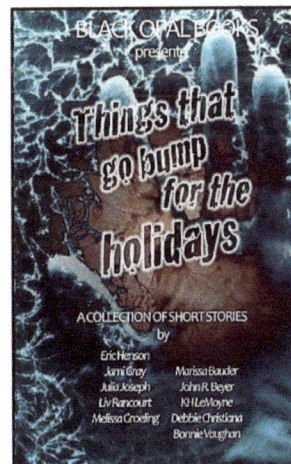

Louise Webb
Letters Member since 1992

The women in Pen Women are inspiring and creative. They are constantly evolving and willing to share their ideas. The group is helpful and supportive in numerous ways. The meetings are always interesting, and I usually learn something new. It is a joy and a privilege to be a member.

I was honored when two of my memoirs, *It's the Inner Beauty That Counts* and *You Can Do It!,* were published in *My Life, My Story, My Legacy, Vintage Wit and Wisdom*, a book of inspiring stories collected by Danni Burton, published by Little White Dog Press.

I have been writing memoirs and leading my own memoirs class for over twenty-one years. *Best of Our Memoirs,* a book featuring and honoring me, compiled and published by Pen Woman and member of the class, Luanna Leisure, contains memoirs from me and the members of my class (available on LuLu.com.)

I began my career as a fourth grade teacher in Riverside, California, subsequently teaching in Hawaii, Santa Barbara, and Saratoga, as well as in France.

I attended Indiana University for two years, National College of Education in Evanston, Illinois, for two years, and, later, after teaching awhile, returned and earned my Master's Degree in Education at National College of Education. It was during this time that I met my husband, Ian, who was attending Northwestern University.

After rearing our daughter, I started a new career as a freelance writer and columnist for the Saratoga News. During my twenty-year career, I had the privilege of interviewing many well-known and prestigious individuals, including Elizabeth Taylor, Willie Nelson, Oprah Winfrey, Olivia de Havilland, Truman Capote, Richard Simmons, Bruce Jenner, Clint Eastwood, Vanna White, Lena Horne, Jimmy Carter, and Gerald Ford. Erma Bombeck once saw some of my writings and wrote to me that I had charisma. For many years, I attended the Oscars to interview the stars.

Above and beyond my writing career, I have run in several marathons (26.2 miles), including one in Russia. I also have an identical twin sister, Susan Gaede of Southern California, who, just like me, taught fourth grade and wrote as a columnist.

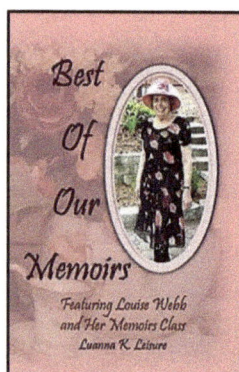

Darlene E. Weingand
Letters and Art Member since 2010

I lived twenty years in Hawaii and was privileged to join the Honolulu branch of the NLAPW as a member in both Letters and Arts. After my husband passed, I no longer had family in Hawaii (although many friends), and I decided to move to a senior-living building in Florence, Oregon. One of my four daughters lived there. I changed my NLAPW membership to member-at-large.

Once Covid-19 hit, familial and social connections switched to Zoom. I met Luanna Leisure at a Zoom meeting. She invited me to join the Santa Clara branch of the NLAPW. I am delighted I did and am very appreciative that their meetings will be hybrid on Zoom.

After doing academic writing during my twenty years as a Professor at the University of Wisconsin-Madison, I retired to Hawaii in 1999. A decade later, I became aware of an interesting fantasy storyline in my mind and began writing it soon after. It was an occasional hobby for another decade, and then the book became impatient with me and seriously nudge me. Since I began "listening" to the book, the writing has been a fun and all-encompassing part of my life. A *Crystal Saga* Series: Books One and Two, *Tamara's Crystals* and *Genesis Explored,* are combined into one book, with more books in the works. Available on LuLu.com and Amazon.com.

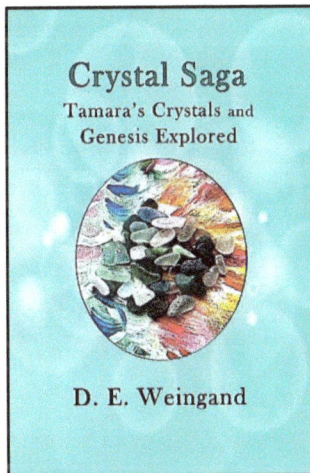

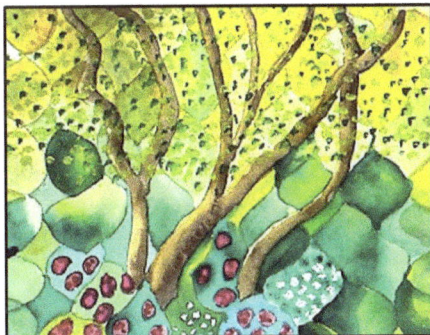

Tina Jones Williams
Letters Member since 2017

When my children were young, I told them "Everything affects everything else." I have seen that notion play out more times than I can count in my lifetime. I am a proud and active member of Alpha Kappa Alpha Sorority, Inc., the first African American sorority, established in 1908. The current Vice-President of the United States is a member.

I share all of this by way of context. It is because I am a member of AKA that I am a member of NLAPW. One of my sorority sisters recommended me to one of her friends, Dorothy Atkins, who happens to be the NLAPW Santa Clara Branch Membership Outreach Chair. Dorothy contacted me and because of her kindness, knowledge, and love for Pen Women, it was an easy decision to join. I continue to be amazed to know that my name appears on the roster with so many women who have done extraordinary things, both now and in the past.

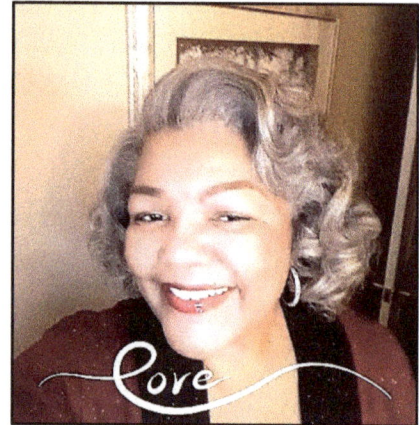

I have been a member only a short time, certainly compared to others, but I have been embraced and supported in my journey as a woman and an author. Pen Women have shared their time, talent, and kind words freely. My life is enriched by being a Pen Woman.

I have written eight books which pay homage to the rich traditions in the African American community. Born and raised in the all-black neighborhood on Julia Street in South Berkeley, I attended neighborhood schools until seventh grade when I was bussed out of my area to become a member of the first desegregated junior high school in Berkeley. I attended Berkeley High, the only public high school in town.

Since publishing my Julia Street Series, I have led bi-annual neighborhood walks which begin and end on Julia Street where the four books are set. During the walks, I share anecdotes, folklore, and history about times, places, and people I feel should not be forgotten. As a result of my books and neighborhood walks, I am pictured on a South Berkeley mural reflecting the city's history. Julia Street is also depicted on the mural and is listed among ten streets considered the "heart of South Berkeley."

There is a plaque with my name and quote had been added to the mosaic at the base of the mural. The mural sits on the bus route my grandmother took twice a day to get to and from her job as a domestic day worker in the Berkeley Hills. "Because she was, I am."

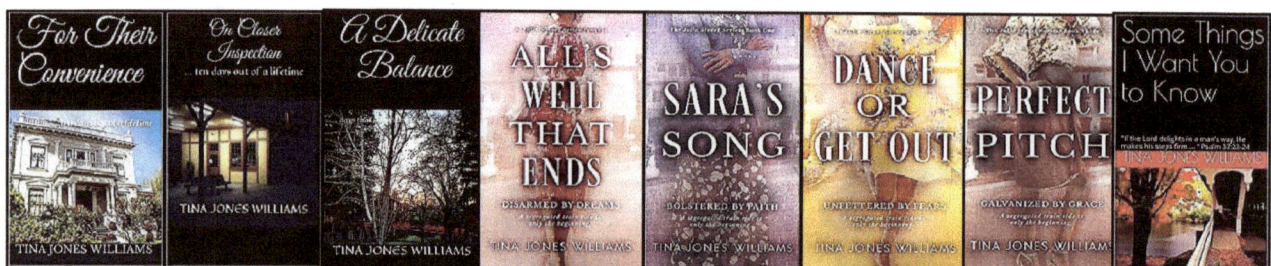

Susan Zerweck
Music Member since 1991

When I was honored to be an Achiever in 1991, Pen Women member, Dorothy Goble, offered to sponsor me to become a member of the Santa Clara County Branch. I was a busy lady at that time, singing professionally, teaching in the Older Adult Program for West Valley & Mission Colleges, a Mary Kay Beauty Consultant plus family responsibilities, so I was reluctant to take on anything else. Luckily for me, I did. It was one of the best decisions I've ever made. To rub shoulders and befriend the most talented and amazing women in the Bay Area, and in the nation, has been so inspiring. It has made me a better musician/composer and a better person. When I attended my first Biennial, I knew I needed to attend every time I am able. It's so much fun to meet the members from all over the U. S. I particularly love our Celebrity Luncheon where we honor talented women who, many times, get no recognition for their work.

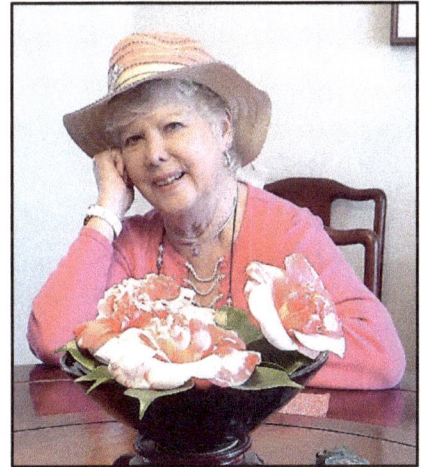

I was born in Greensburg, Pennsylvania, a 150 year old town 32 miles east of Pittsburgh. My Dad was a one-room schoolteacher, but eventually managed an Esso Station, as teaching didn't even pay enough for a family with one child. It was a lovely place to grow up with lots of freedom to explore and neighbors to watch over me. My parents divorced the summer before my 9th birthday and after Mother married my step-father we traveled all over the Eastern and Southern United States for his business. We lived in a 31 x 8 ft. trailer, which made it much easier to move quickly.

I was 12 ½ when my brother Robert was born in Memphis, TN. The trailer became quite crowded, so after moving to Columbus Ohio at the end of my 7th grade, we purchased a house in the suburb of Worthington. Graduating from Worthington High School in 1957 made it the 13th school I had attended. That same summer we moved to Long Beach, California, but my parents decided Menlo Park was where they wanted to put down roots. While working in San Diego at the family business, I met my 1st husband, Steve Foster, just finishing a 20 year career in the Navy. We lived in Louisiana, Texas, then Northern California, moving to the Santa Cruz Mountains in 1968 amd built our home. After 10 years of marriage and no children, we had a wonderful opportunity to adopt our daughter, Robin, at 4 days old in 1969. Nine months and one day later I gave birth to son, Brian.

Steve and I divorced after 16 years of marriage in 1974 and I met and married Ralph Zerweck in 1975. We have been married 46 ½ years and he has been a wonderful father to my children and grandchildren. He has 2 children and 2 grandchildren. We both love living in our beautiful mountains in the house that Ralph designed and built himself, which we finished together before our wedding.

I have sung all my life with my first solo in church at age 3. My professional singing as Susan Zee took off after my 2nd marriage and I was blessed to work with many wonderful musicians. I taught Music Appreciation for 13 years in the Older Adult Program for West Valley and Mission Colleges. At age 70 my voice began to have problems, so decided it was time to retire. I do miss it a lot and no longer write songs as I have no place to perform them. I wrote all my own shows which were mostly an hour long for conventions, clubs, banquets, etc. and sang for hundreds of weddings and many funerals. It was a wonderful career.

Guess Who
Revealed

Page 73

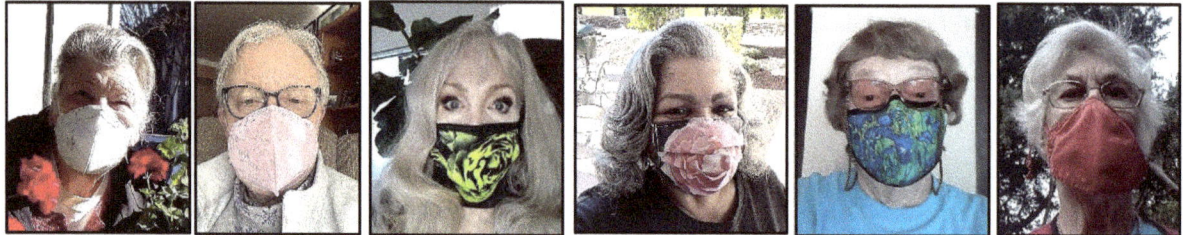

Carol Brolin	Darlene Weingand	Jeanne Carbone	Tina Jones Williams	Alice Ann Glenn	Kay Duffy

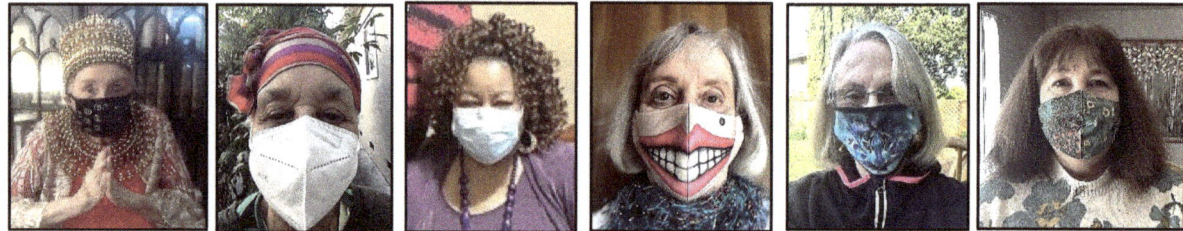

Audry Lynch	Dorothy Atkins	Gerri Forté	Carol Greene	Patricia Dennis	Lorraine Gabbert

Page 74

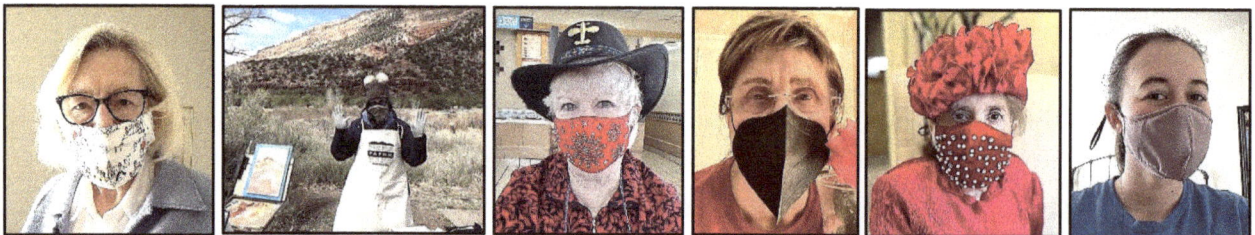

Ursula Meier	Phyllis Gunderson	Susan Zerweck	Sheralee Iglehart	Louise Webb	Janie Oberhauser

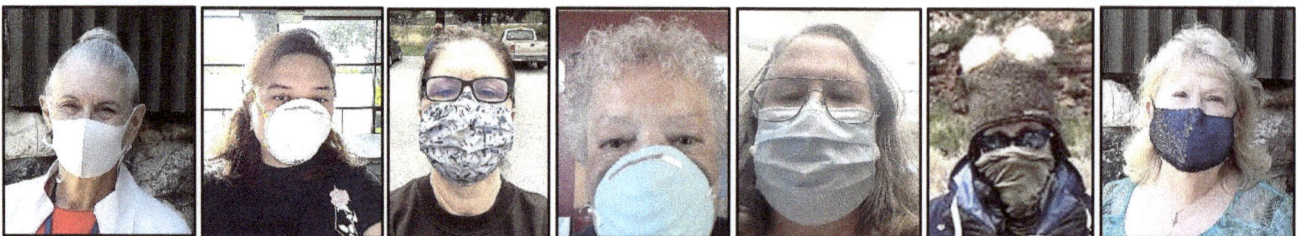

Rolayne Edwards	Genevieve Liu	Marcia Sivek	Pat Fisher	Gail Lockhart	Phyllis Gunderson	Luanna Leisure

In Memoriam
To Honor and Remember

Dorothy Goble
1914 - 2012

Maryhill Gleason
1916 - 2021

Felicia Pollock
1921 - 2014

Erna Holyer
1925 - 2007

Doris Phifer
1928 - 2018

Vallie Chan
1932 - 2015

Nancy Bloomer
Deussen
1932- 2019

Judy Bingman
1940 - 2019

Judith
Oppenheimer
1940 - 2021

Toni Hird
1943 - 2015

Brenda Elliott
1945 - 2018

Visits from National Presidents

National Presidents
C. 2018
It has been our privilege and honor to have visits for our Celebrity Luncheons by three of our National Presidents. Candace Long at the microphone, Virginia Campbell to the left and Evelyn Wofford. Photo to the left taken by Anne Baehr.

Candace Long, National President
February 6, 2015
Left to right: Mary Lou Taylor, Luanna Leisure, Candace Long, Louise Webb, Edie Matthews, Maralyn Miller.

Virginia Campbell, National President
February 11, 2017
Left to right: Patricia Dennis, Judy Bingman, Nancy Bloomer Deussen, Katy Tyler, Virginia Campbell, Susan Zerweck.

Evelyn Wofford, National President
Feb. 1, 2020
Left to right: Carol Greene, Louise Webb, Dorothy Atkins, Susan Zerweck, Norma Slavit, Evelyn Wofford, Patricia Dennis, ShaRon Haugen, Cyra Cowan.

We Are Pen Women
Northern California
Branches

NorCal
Northern California Branches

What is NorCal?

NorCal is: The five NLAPW branches in Northern California:
1. Diablo-Alameda Branch
2. Golden Gate-Marin Branch
3. Modesto Branch
4. Santa Clara County Branch
5. Stockton-Lodi Branch

NorCal Officers:
President: Dorothy Atkins
Vice President: Luanna Leisure
Secretary: Caroline Henry
Treasurer: Barbara Chamberlain
NorCal Facebook Host: Luanna Leisure
NorCal Newsletter: Jill Adler

We meet twice a year and during these meeting we try to include all genres. We have literary contests and art shows. During Covid-19 we have been able to connect more often using zoom.

The purpose of NorCal is to keep us connected so we can get to know one another, encourage, support, mentor and share our talents. These are the ties that bind. It is uplifting to meet with like-minded sisters in our Northern California Branches.

Our NorCal Facebook page is another way of promoting all NorCal branches. Our NorCal Facebook page title is: NorCal NLAPW.

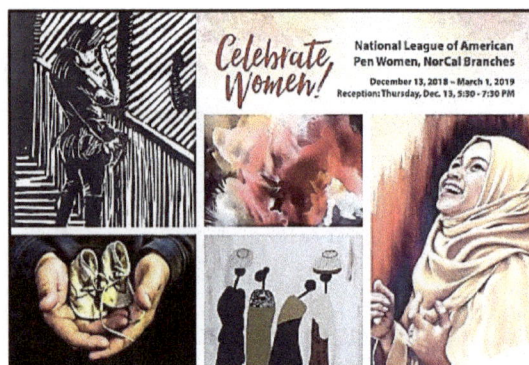

History of
Northern California Branches

The first Northern California Branch was established in San Francisco in 1916. Five of the original 15 are still active.

1. 1916: San Francisco
2. **1922: Santa Clara County**
3. 1925: Sacramento
4. 1926: Butte County
5. 1927: Sonoma County
6. **1936: Modesto**
7. **1950: Diablo-Alameda**
8. **1950: Stockton San Joaquin (Now Stockton-Lodi)**
9. **1972: Golden Gate-Marin County**
10. 1973: Santa Cruz
11. 1981: Nob Hill San Francisco
12. 1981: Carmel by the Sea
13. 1982: Napa Valley
14. 1987: Las Artes (Palo Alto)
15. 1996: Lake Tahoe (South Lake Tahoe)

Celebrate Women!

National League of American Pen Women, NorCal Branches

October 6 through November 17, 2017
Reception: Friday, October 6, 5:30 - 7:30 PM

**NorCal Meeting
Art Contest Winners
2012
Hosted by Santa Clara
County Branch**

Felicia Pollock
Dianne Glass MacNair
Louise Webb
Judy Bingman

**NorCal Meeting 2017
Letters Contest Winners
Hosted by Modesto Branch**

Dorothy Atkins, Luanna Leisure, Louise Kantro, Linda Sawyer, Ann Bailey,
Linda Prather-Nelson, Barbara Chamberlain, Kathie Isaac-Luke

NorCal Meeting 2016
Hosted by Diablo-Alameda Branch
at the Home of Winifred Thompson

Back Row Left to Right: Judy Bingman, Christine Horner, Joan Booséy, Elizabeth Hack, Name Unknown, Barbara Chamberlain, Caroline Henry, Genie Lester, Dorothy Atkins, Dori Pendergrass, Susan Taira as Charlie Chaplin, President Diablo-Alameda Branch, Winifred Thompson, Jo Ann Frisch, Jill Adler, Lynn Hansen, Natica Angilly, Debbie Patrick, ShaRon Haugen, Luanna Leisure.

Above Owl perched on a stump in Winifred's back yard.

NorCal Meeting Spring 2018
Hosted by Modesto Branch
at the Home of Jill Adler

Back Row Left to Right: Luanna Leisure, Loretta Ichord, Henrietta Sparkman, Guest, Modesto President, Louise Kantro, Dorothy Atkins, Lisa Bruk, Ann Bailey
Middle Left to Right: Barbara Chamberlain, Pat Fisher, Nancy Bloomer Deussen, Jill Adler
Front Row Left to Right: Dianne Glass MacNair, ShaRon Haugen, Pat Egenberger, Not pictured, Cleo Griffith.

Cleo Griffith

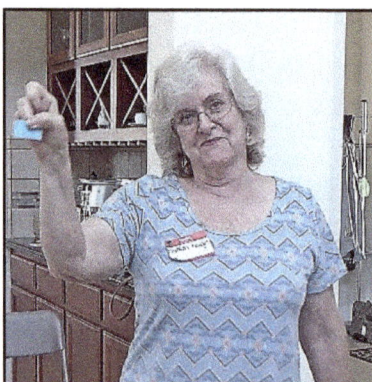

ShaRon Haugen

Barbara Chamberlain, Lisa Bruk, Nancy Bloomer Deussen

NorCal Luncheon for National President Evelyn Wofford
February 8, 2019
Hosted by Diablo-Alameda Branch

Back Row Left to Right: Luanna Leisure, Judy Bingman, Connie Rusk, Debra Collins, Doris Nikolaidis, National President, Evelyn Wofford, Jo Ann Frisch, Diablo-Alameda President, Winifred Thompson, Pam Holloway, Ann Maloney-Mason
Front Row Left to Right: Carol Markos, Susan Zerweck, Usha Shukla, Dorothy Atkins, ShaRon Haugen

Four Presidents
Luanna Leisure, Santa Clara County Branch
Winifred Thompson, Diablo-Alameda Branch
Evenlyn Wofford, National President
Dorothy Atkins, NorCal

National President, Evelyn Wofford
holding photo by Judy Bingman which
she won in the raffle.

NorCal Meeting
June 8, 2019
Hosted by Stockton-Lodi Branch

Back Row Left to Right: Patricia Mayorga, Patricia Kennedy, guest speaker Renee Rondon, Cleo Griffith, Lynn Hansen, Nora Dale, Carol David, Chella Gonsalves, Luanna Leisure
Front Row Left to Right: Jill Adler, Modesto President, Caroline Henry, Audry Lynch, ShaRon Haugen, Dorothy Atkins, Louise Kantro, Barbara Chamberlain, Donna Sordyl

Front to Back Left: Lynn Hansen, Carol David, Caroline Henry,
Front to Back Right: Cleo Griffith, Chella Gonsalves, Nora Dale
Picture to the Right: Jill Adler

NorCal Zoom
Hosted by Golden Gate-Marin Branch
June 6, 2020
Dorothy Atkins Guest Speaker
Social Justice from the Perspective of a Pen Woman of Color

Top row: Cathy Moreno, Patricia Dennis, Debbie Patrick; Branch President, Lucy Arnold, Luanna Leisure
2nd Row: Rita Wienk, NorCal President, Dorothy Atkins, Elizabeth Lauer, Melissa Woodburn, Joan Booséy
3rd Row: Anita Nelson, Linda Larsen, Alice Ann Glenn, Susan Zerweck, Karen Franzenburg
4th row: Joyce Andrade, Donna Solin, Jane Liston, Lorraine Gabbert

NorCal

Art Creating Community
NorCal in Person and Zoom
Reception - December 8, 2021
Hosted by Golden Gate-Marin Branch

Art Creating Community

Linda Larson was Chair and Marin-Golden Gate Branch and President, Lucy Arnold, hosted the "Art Creating Community" NorCal exhibition at the Lindsay Dirkx Brown Gallery in San Ramon, California. The Diablo-Alameda Branch President, Winifred Thompson, and members helped organize the event and enjoyed zooming with National President, Evelyn Wofford, and other NorCal members at the reception.

Above Photo:
Left to right: Margaret Davis, Connie Rusk, Winifred Thompson, Jo Ann Frisch, Usha Shukla, Ruey Syrup, Charlotte Severin, Pamela Holloway

We Are Pen Women
Washington, D.C.

Let's Start at the Beginning

The Santa Clara County Branch would not be in existence if it were not for the brave, determined, and talented women who came before us. Let's take a walk down history road and cover National in Washington, D.C.

"Pen Women of this millennium are stewards of the legacy envisioned by those seventeen progressive pioneers. Their vision has carried the organization into a future "The Dauntless Three" could hardly have imagined."

The Rise of Pen Women – 1897

On a humid Saturday evening in June of 1897, William McKinley enjoyed a quiet dinner at the White House. Three months earlier, he had declared in his inaugural address that, "...equality of rights must prevail." A few blocks away on Rhode Island Avenue were seventeen women to whom those words rang hollow. It was not the vote, however, that occupied these ladies, but problems peculiar to "the writer's craft:" libel and copyright laws, plagiarism and the inequality with which professionals of "the fair sex" were treated by their male counterparts. (Read more in "Fighting for the Right to Write" by Siggy Buckley, Jacksonville, Florida Branch.)

This first meeting of The League of American Pen Women was organized by Marian Longfellow O'Donoghue (yes, Henry's niece), who wrote for newspapers in Washington D.C. and Boston. She invited fellow journalists Margaret Sullivan Burke and Anna Sanborn Hamilton to join her in establishing a "progressive press union" for the female writers of Washington.

"The Dauntless Three" brought together seventeen women: writers, novelists, newspaper women, a teacher, a poet and an artist. They hoped that these "active pen women" would find in the group, "mutual aid, advice, and future development" for each other and their careers (quotes from The League Minutes, 26 June, 1897).

Professional credentials were required for membership and the ladies determined that Pen Women should always be paid for their work. Artists and composers were welcomed by their literary sisters. By September of 1898, the League boasted over fifty members "from Maine to Texas, from New York to California."

composers from the National League of American Pen Women
Washington DC, April 1932

The association became The National League of American Pen Women in 1921 with thirty-five local branches in various states. Membership increased

through the '20s and '30s. First ladies have traditionally been awarded honorary membership and on occasion have actively participated in League functions. Eleanor Roosevelt, a prolific writer, was an enthusiastic Pen Woman during her tenure in the White House and beyond.

Social events hosted by the League and attended by the Washington elite became highlights of the Season and raised funds for League properties and projects. National conventions began in the early 1920's and have continued as biennials alternating between Washington D.C. and other cities around the nation.

The Pen Woman magazine debuted in 1920 and continued until 1923 when The Official Bulletin was substituted for the periodical. In 1940, *The Pen Woman* reemerged as the organization's journal and vehicle for members' creative works and League communications.

In the ensuing years, writing competitions, art exhibitions, and special events showcased the works not only of League members, but aspiring artists, writers and musicians. Scholarships for students and mature women honing their craft have been hallmarks of League efforts.

The League is headquartered in the historic Pen Arts Building in the DuPont Circle area of Washington, D. C.

The U.S. population has more than tripled since the birth of the League. More than a decade into its second century, 55,000 writers, artists and musicians have been proud to call themselves Pen Women. Many of the battles fought by the founders have largely been won, but other challenges remain. For professional women, parity with men in the workplace is still a goal to be achieved.

Pen Women of this millennium are stewards of the legacy envisioned by those seventeen progressive pioneers. Their vision has carried the organization into a future "The Dauntless Three" could hardly have imagined.

There is much yet to be done as we turn our attention to an expanded mission. Mentoring, encouraging and promoting emerging professional women in the arts is incumbent upon current members.

The above article is from our NLAPW.org website. Permission was granted to use this article. Author unknown.

Charter Members
Washington, D. C.
1897

Abby Gunn Baker
Mary Temple Bayard
Margaret Sullivan Burke
Ada Tower Cable
Jennie S. Campbell
Mary Andrews Denison
Mattie Hamilton Flick
Virginia King Frye
Anna Sanborn Hamilton
Tillie Orr Hays
Nannie M. Lancaster
Marian Longfellow (O'Donoghue)
Alice R. Morgan
Anna B. Patten
Belle Vane Sherwood
Emma V. Triepel   Margaret Wade

composers from the National League of American Pen Women
Washington DC, April 1932

Left: Pen Women Composers, Washington D.C. April 1932

Right: Charter Members document hanging in the Pen Arts Building Washington, D.C. Photo taken by National President, Evelyn Wofford

General Information
Taken from the National League of American Pen Women, Inc.
Washington, D. C. Roster 2000-2002

MOTTO:

"All for one, and one for all." The quotation is taken from Alexandre Dumas in *The Three Musketeers*, and was suggested as the Pen Woman's motto in 1897 by Marian Longfellow.

FLOWER:

The Red Rose

COLORS:

Red, White, and Blue, a patriotic color theme was adopted by the charter members during a period of American expansion.

INSIGNIA:

The "wisdom" of the Owl was an important consideration in choosing the insignia. The first sketch was designed by the only artist in the original group, Alice R. Morgan.

Coins Minted
In 1897

Morgan Silver Dollar
1897

Half Dollar

Quarter Dollar

One Dime

V Cents

One Cent

A Few Historical Events
1897-98

Jan 10 Ukrainian bacteriologist Wademar Haffkine performs the first human trial for a vaccine for the plague on himself during the Bombay epidemic.

Jan 11 M H Cannon becomes 1st woman state senator in US (Utah)

January 23 Elva Zona Heaster is found dead in Greenbrier County, West Virginia. The resulting murder trial of her husband is perhaps the only case in United States history where the alleged testimony of a ghost helped secure a conviction.

March 4 William McKinley was inaugurated as president of the United States.

July The Klondike Gold Rush began in Alaska.

When the stampede that was the *Klondike gold rush* occurred in late 1897, women had already spent the decade striving for independence. Employment, fashion and recreation had been their soundboard to proclaim this ideal. The Klondike provided a chance for individual women to prove they were capable of anything.

February 15, 1898 The American battleship U.S.S. Maine exploded in the harbor at Havana, Cuba, a mysterious event that led to the United States going to war with Spain.

National Board of Directors
January 18, 2022

National Board of Directors
January 18, 2022

Top left to right: Susan Zerweck, Commemorative Endowment Chair; Luanna Leisure, Membership Development Chair; Sandra Michael, Archives; Lucy Arnold, Publications; Joan Applebaum, National Art Chair.

2nd row: Candace Long, Treasurer; Jessica Rigouard, Governance; Laura Walth, Fifth Vice President; Janie Owens, Recording Secretary; Evelyn Wofford, National President.

3rd row: Marjorie Vaughan, Parliamentarian; Nancy Dafoe, Vinnie Ream Chair; Sheila Byrnes, First Vice President; Reverend Robin Moscati, Chaplain; Kathy Pate, National Music;

Bottom row: Nancy Kyme, Outreach; Mary Patricia Canes, Fourth Vice President, not pictured Lorna Jean Hagstrom, Third Vice President.

Not in Photo
Special Elected Position, Alice Ann Glenn, Ethics Board Chair
Rodika Tollefson, Editor-in-Chief, The Pen Woman, Web Editor

National Pen Arts Building
1300 17th Street, N.W., Washington, D.C. 2003-1901

Judy Bingman
Santa Clara County Branch Member
Judy's favorite place to sit in the
Pen Arts Building was in the Parlor by the
windows.
Library to the left

Pen Arts Building Photo Tour
Continued

Little Morning Glory
Marble Bust
By Vinnie Ream

Diana the hunter
Sculpture
By Bertina

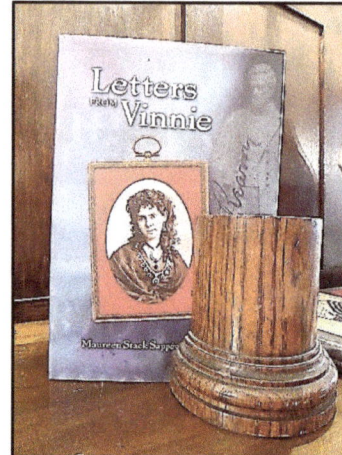

The Parlor

Luanna Leisure,
Guest from Foreign Embassy,
National President,
Virginia Campbell

Pen Arts Building Photo Tour
Continued

Stairs, Stairs,
and More Stairs

Performance of a Nancy Bloomer Deussen Composition

Luanna Leisure
Prior to presentation

Judy Bingman, Luanna Leisure, Laura Walth, Ronni Miller

Until We Meet Again
Evelyn Wofford, Judy Bingman, Elaine Waidelich, Name Unknown. Luanna Leisure

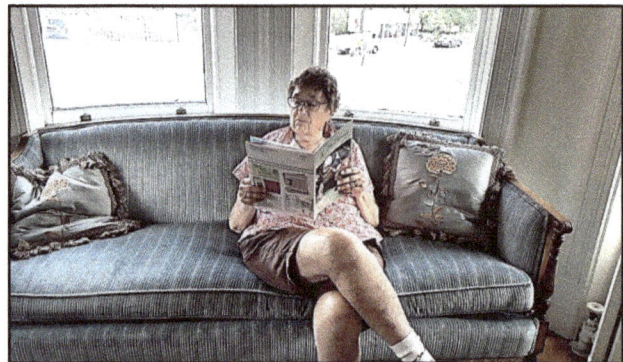

National Biennial Convention

The League holds a Biennial Convention in March or April of the even numbered years, unless it is agreed by a 2/3 (two-thirds) vote of the Board of Directors that a justifiable reason exists for cancellation of the convention. The Biennial Convention takes place in a city where a branch has extended an invitation and has agreed to host the Biennial.

Because of the Covid-19 Pandemic, the Biennial Convention has been postponed three times. The 50th Biennial is now scheduled for April 20 – May 1, 2022 in Washington, D.C.

The National League of American Pen Women, Inc.

Presents the

LETTERS CONTEST WINNERS
FOR THE

2002 BIENNIAL CONVENTION

APRIL 10-15 IN SAN FRANCISCO, CA

MARJORIE DAVIS ROLLER NON-FICTION

1st Place
AUDRY L. LYNCH
Santa Clara Branch, CA.
"Steinbeck Remembered"

2nd Place
JUNE M.F. WILDEMAN
Atlanta Branch, Ga.
"Breaking the Sound Barrier"

3rd Place
DOROTHY KAMM
Treasure Coast Branch. Fla.
"Painted Porcelain Jewelry & Buttons

C. NORMAN & MARJORIE J. ROLLER

1st Place
DEE ANN PALMER
San Bernardino Valley, Branch, CA.
"Aquatic Equine"

2nd Place
GAYLYNN LANKFORD, Ph.D
Jacksonville, Fla.
"The Squirrel's Rescuer's Handbook"

**2002
Biennial Letters
Contest Winner**

Audry Lynch
Wins 1st Place

*"Steinback
Remembered"*
The Marjorie Davis
Roller Non-Fiction
Award

National Biennial Convention

**NLAPW Biennial
April 10-15, 2002
San Francisco**

Hosted by the Santa Clara
County Branch

Sharon Haugen, Maria Chaviel,
Doris Phifer, Bea Warren,
Christine Dargahi, Felica Pollock,
Susan Zerweck

**NLAPW Biennial
April 10-15, 2002 - San Francisco**

Back left to right: Jerri Scaife, Carol Greene, Vallie Chan, Toni Hird, Cleo McDowell
Front left to right: Susan Zerweck, ShaRon Haugen, Beatrice Warren, Felicia Pollock

National Biennial Convention

2016 Biennial
Judy Bingman receives photography award.

2018 Biennial
Swimming Upstream forum, Brig. Gen Clara Adams, Moderator. Panel: Bonnie Jo Smith, Gail Speckmann, Nancy Bloomer Deussen, Jeannie Hope Gibson, and Kelly Ann Compton. Photo by Laura Walth.

The panel was about people who have gone through trauma and mental health issues and came through the other side.

Santa Clara County Branch members, Bonnie Jo Smith and Nancy Bloomer Deussen. Bonnie's textile is in the overhead image.

NLAPW Biennial Updated Schedule of Events
Thursday, April 28 – Sunday, May 1, 2022
The Darcy, 1515 Rhode Island Ave. NW, Washington, DC

Thursday, April 28, 2022
Arrive at conference hotel

4-5:30 p.m.	2020-2022 Board of Directors Meeting @ The Darcy
5-7 p.m.	Registration @ The Darcy, second floor

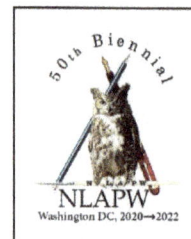

Dinner on your own

Friday, April 29 @ The Darcy

7:30-8:30 a.m.	Registration @ The Darcy, second floor
8:30-9:30 a.m.	*Master Calligrapher Demonstration,* Riva Brown
8:30-9:30 a.m.	*Novel Writing Workshop: Grab My Attention and Hold It,* Nancy Dafoe, National Letters Chair
10-11 a.m.	*Memoir Writing Workshop: Finding Your Personal Treasures,* Margaret McMullan
10-11 a.m.	*Ekphrastic Writing: How It Works and Why It Is Important for Visual Artists, Writers, and All the Arts,* Central New York Branch Members
11:30 a.m.-1 p.m.	**Art Luncheon** at The Darcy, Guest Speaker and Art Judge Renee Sandell
1:30-4:30 p.m.	**Business Meeting** (all Pen Women)
6:45-9 p.m.	**Vinnie Ream Banquet and Awards,** Guest Speaker Ann B. Friedman (all attendees)

Saturday, April 30 @ Pen Arts

9-10 a.m.	*From Genesis to Theatrical Presentation,* Patricia Black-Gould, Barbara J. Dunham, Sheila Firestone
10:30-11:30 a.m.	*Turning Points Panel Discussion,* Moderator Jamie Tate with Sheila M. Byrnes and Grace Reid

Lunch on your own

2-3:30 p.m.	**Music Performance and Music Awards**
3:30-4:30 p.m.	Music Reception, hosted by the Central New York and D.C. branches
4:30-6 p.m.	Biennial Art Exhibition @ Pen Arts Gallery

Dinner on your own

8 p.m.	A Reading with Biennial Winners @ The Darcy, Nancy Dafoe, National Letters Chair

Sunday, May 1 @ The Darcy

8:30-9:30 a.m.	*Right Down to the Nitty Gritty, Preparing Your Manuscript,* National Letters Chair Nancy Dafoe and National Publications Chair Lucy Arnold
8:30-9:30 a.m.	*How to Market Your Art to Corporations, Organizations, and City Leaders,* Beverly Goldie
10-11 a.m.	TBA
10-11 a.m.	*Documenting Experience through Urban Sketching,* Susan Murphy
11:30 a.m.-1 p.m.	**Letters Luncheon,** Guest Speaker Karen Pastorello
1:30-2:30 p.m.	*Historical Fiction,* Irish author Mary Pat Kelly
1:30-2:30 p.m.	*Recharging Your Creativity with Alcohol Inks,* Joan Applebaum, National Art Chair
3-3:45 p.m.	Memorial by the Rev. Robin J. Moscati, National Chaplain
3:45-4 p.m.	Introduction of New Members by Luanna Leisure, National Membership Development Chair
4:00-4:15 p.m.	Closing Remarks by National President Evelyn B. Wofford
4:45-5:15 p.m.	Installation of incoming NLAPW Officers by the Rev. Robin J. Moscati
5:15-6:15 p.m.	Closing: *Watching History Come to Life, Woman Justices of the Supreme Court,* Trish Chambers

Dinner on your own

Monday, May 2

9:30-11 a.m.	2022-2024 Board of Directors Business Meeting @ The Darcy

Index

164

S

Severin, Charlotte 146
Shannon, Alice R. 14
Sheen, Jeanna 72
Sheppard, Melody 52
Shernock, Judith 34, 53
Sherwood, Belle Vane 150
Sherwood, Patricia 52
Shukla, Usha ix, 143, 146
Simmons, Doris 15
Simpkins, Pearl H. 14
Sinclair, Micach 72
Sivek, Marcia 16, 18, 19, 21, 24, 26, 29, 34, 35, 36, 39, 45, 53, 67, 70, 74, 120,134
Skerry-Olsen, Eva 5,
Slavit, Norma 23, 29, 31, 37, 43, 47, 48, 49, 53, 63, 66, 121, 136
Smart, Ariel 21, 70, 122
Smith, Bonnie Jo 37, 53, 123, 161
Smith, Vema Moxley 14
Solin, Donna 145
Sordyl, Donna 144
Sparkman, Henrietta 142
Speckmann, Gail 161
Spencer, Priscilla 57
Staschower, Paul 43
Stetson, Bob 26,
Su, Jing-Shi 63, 64
Suggs, Patricia, 32, 124
Syrup, Ruey ix, 146
Swairsky, Sandy 62

T

Tan, Annette 18, 34, 53,
Taira, Susan 141
Taylor, Mary Lou 9, 21, 33, 44, 58, 60, 65, 104, 125,136
Taylor, Tyler 64
Tegner, Thyra 15
Thompson, Lori Howell 50, 126
Thompson, Winifred vii, ix, 141, 143, 146
Tillman, Jeanne 53

T

Tinsley, Barbara 54
Tolbot, Ester 51
Tollefson, Rodika 153
Tolley, Jude vii, 2, 4, 18, 20, 21, 22, 23, 27, 31, 35, 127
Torokhova, Julia 72
Triepel, Emma V. 150
Tyler, Kathryn 15, 18, 19, 21, 24, 31, 34, 35, 36, 39, 45, 46, 49, 60, 65, 128, 136

U

Urban, Catherine 14

V

Vahia, Ushma 53
Van Hart, Holly 54
Van Hoy, Christine 53
Vaughan, Bonnie 18, 19, 24, 33, 60, 129
Vaughan, Marjorie 153
Voth, Norma 71
Vujevich, Raven 72

W

Wacholz, Stanley 51
Wade, Margaret 150
Waidelich, Elaine 158
Walke, Katelynn 72
Walker, Madam C. J. 58
Walth, Laura ix, 153, 158
Warren, Beatrice 71, 160
Watson, Julia 53
Webb, Louise xi, 22, 24, 27, 29, 32, 36, 47, 48, 49, 58, 62, 63, 64, 65, 66, 74, 104,130,134, 136, 140
Weingand, Darlene 29, 37, 62, 73, 131, 134
Wienk, Rita 145
Wildeman, June M. F. 159
Williams, Alma Lowry 14
Williams, Elizabeth Yahn 29
Williams, Tina Jones 16, 21, 29, 31, 37, 53, 66, 70, 73, 132

W

Wofford, Evelyn vii, viii, ix, 32, 46, 47, 48, 49, 50, 136, 143, 153, 158
Wong, Audrey 25
Woodburn, Melissa 145

X

Y

Yang, Denise 57

Z

Zerweck, Ralph 26, 45
Zerweck, Susan vii, 3, 15, 16, 18, 19, 23, 24, 25, 26, 27, 31, 32, 34, 35, 36, 37, 45, 46, 47, 48, 49, 50, 53, 54, 55, 58, 71, 74, 133, 134, 136, 143, 145, 153, 160

www.ingramcontent.com/pod-product-compliance
Lightning Source LLC
Chambersburg PA
CBHW041801280326
41926CB00103B/4768